BEFORE HOUDINI

BEFORE HOUDINI

WRITTEN BY
JEREMY HOLT

ILLUSTRATED BY
JOHN LUCAS

COLORS BY
ADI CROSSA

LETTERED BY
A LARGER WORLD STUDIOS

INSIGHT
COMICS

San Rafael, California

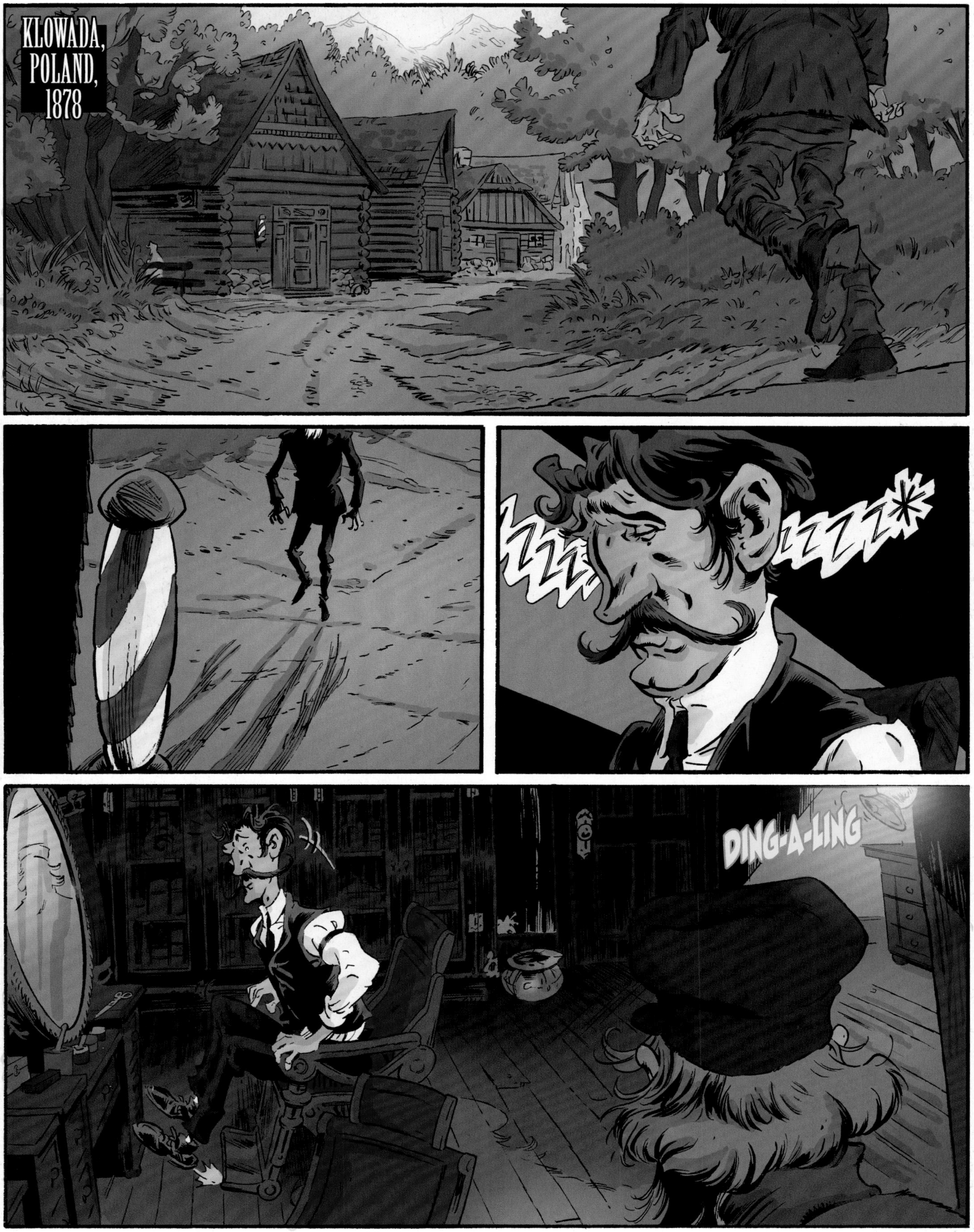
KLOWADA, POLAND, 1878
ZZZZ
ZZZZZ
DING-A-LING

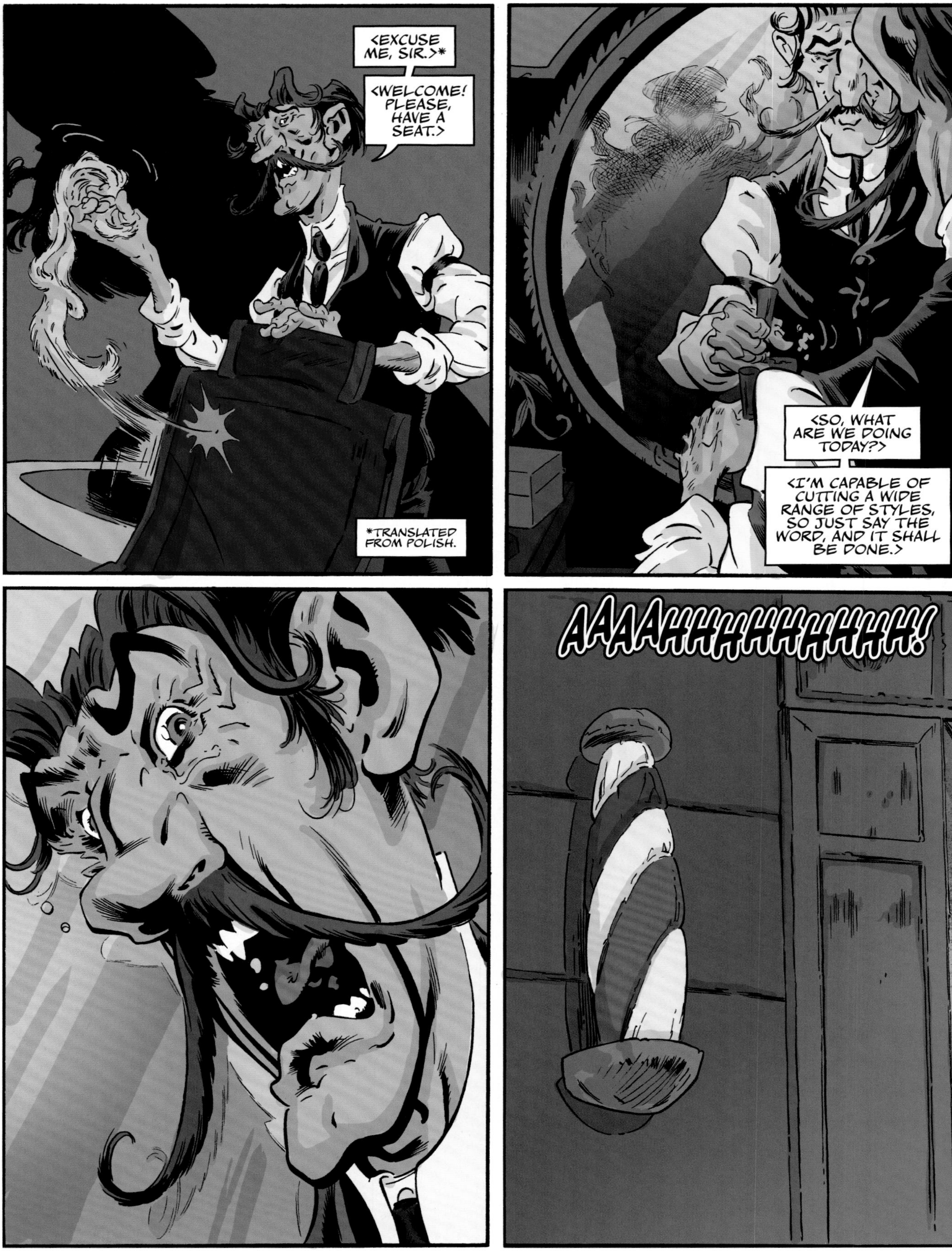
<EXCUSE ME, SIR.>*
<WELCOME! PLEASE, HAVE A SEAT.>
*TRANSLATED FROM POLISH.
<SO, WHAT ARE WE DOING TODAY?>
<I'M CAPABLE OF CUTTING A WIDE RANGE OF STYLES, SO JUST SAY THE WORD, AND IT SHALL BE DONE.>
AAAAHHHHHHHHH!

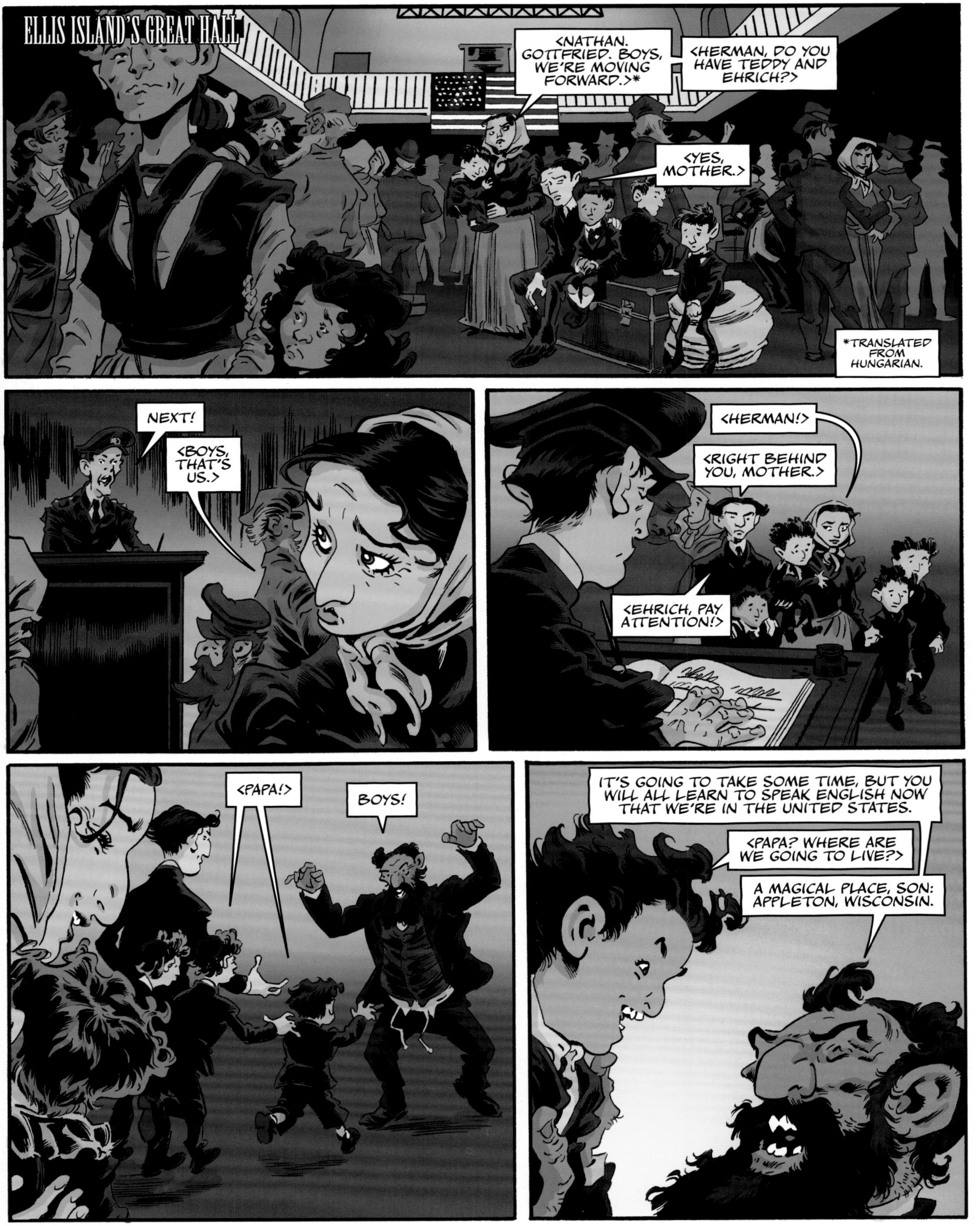
ELLIS ISLAND'S GREAT HALL
<NATHAN. GOTTFRIED. BOYS, WE'RE MOVING FORWARD.>*
<HERMAN, DO YOU HAVE TEDDY AND EHRICH?>
<YES, MOTHER.>
*TRANSLATED FROM HUNGARIAN.
NEXT!
<BOYS, THAT'S US.>
<HERMAN!>
<RIGHT BEHIND YOU, MOTHER.>
<EHRICH, PAY ATTENTION!>
<PAPA!>
BOYS!
IT'S GOING TO TAKE SOME TIME, BUT YOU WILL ALL LEARN TO SPEAK ENGLISH NOW THAT WE'RE IN THE UNITED STATES.
<PAPA? WHERE ARE WE GOING TO LIVE?>
A MAGICAL PLACE, SON: APPLETON, WISCONSIN.

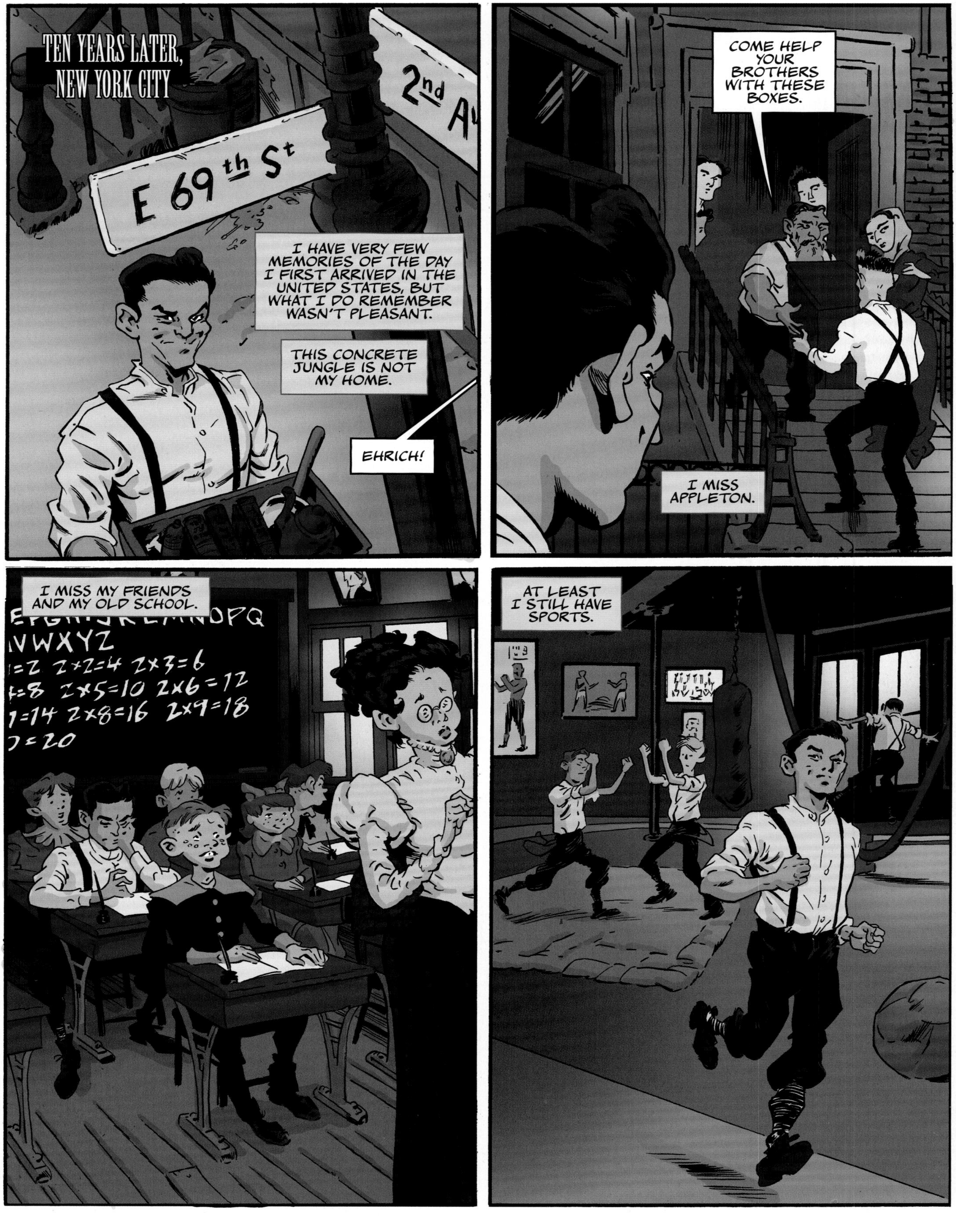
TEN YEARS LATER, NEW YORK CITY
E 69th St
2nd Av
I HAVE VERY FEW MEMORIES OF THE DAY I FIRST ARRIVED IN THE UNITED STATES, BUT WHAT I DO REMEMBER WASN'T PLEASANT.
THIS CONCRETE JUNGLE IS NOT MY HOME.
EHRICH!
COME HELP YOUR BROTHERS WITH THESE BOXES.
I MISS APPLETON.
I MISS MY FRIENDS AND MY OLD SCHOOL.
AT LEAST I STILL HAVE SPORTS.

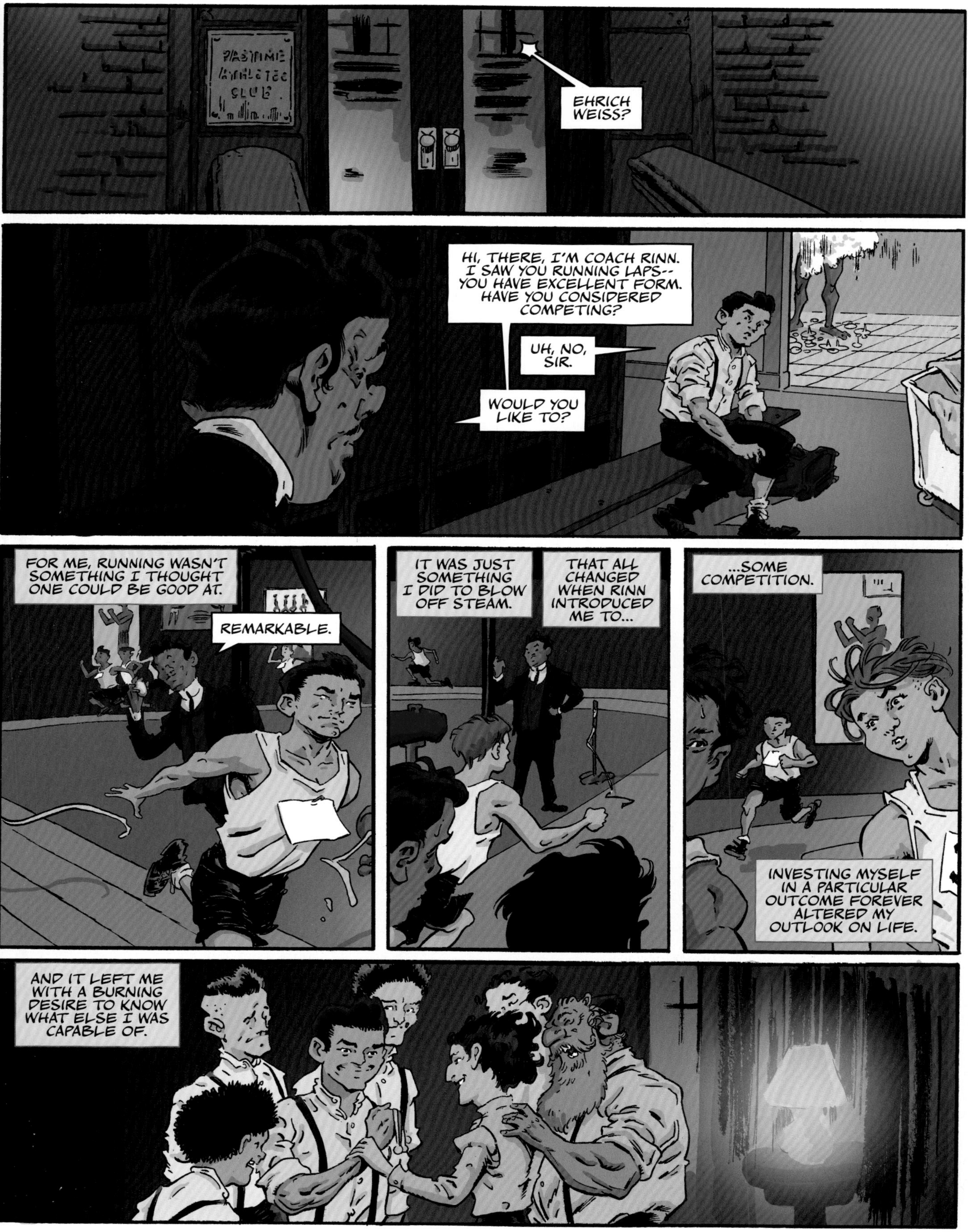
PASTIME ATHLETIC CLUB
EHRICH WEISS?
HI, THERE, I'M COACH RINN. I SAW YOU RUNNING LAPS-- YOU HAVE EXCELLENT FORM. HAVE YOU CONSIDERED COMPETING?
UH, NO, SIR.
WOULD YOU LIKE TO?
FOR ME, RUNNING WASN'T SOMETHING I THOUGHT ONE COULD BE GOOD AT.
REMARKABLE.
IT WAS JUST SOMETHING I DID TO BLOW OFF STEAM.
THAT ALL CHANGED WHEN RINN INTRODUCED ME TO...
...SOME COMPETITION.
INVESTING MYSELF IN A PARTICULAR OUTCOME FOREVER ALTERED MY OUTLOOK ON LIFE.
AND IT LEFT ME WITH A BURNING DESIRE TO KNOW WHAT ELSE I WAS CAPABLE OF.

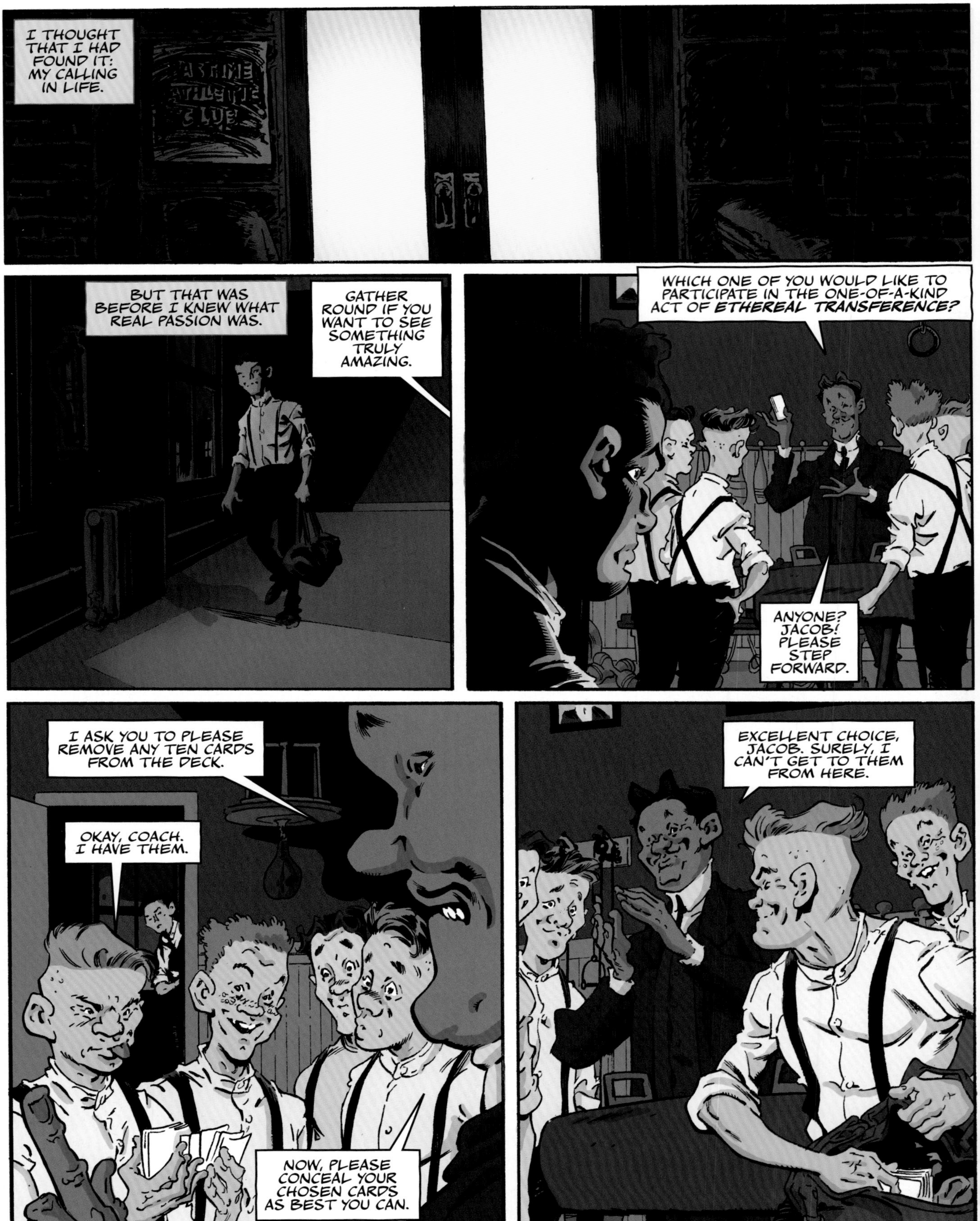
I THOUGHT THAT I HAD FOUND IT: MY CALLING IN LIFE.
BUT THAT WAS BEFORE I KNEW WHAT REAL PASSION WAS.
GATHER ROUND IF YOU WANT TO SEE SOMETHING TRULY AMAZING.
WHICH ONE OF YOU WOULD LIKE TO PARTICIPATE IN THE ONE-OF-A-KIND ACT OF *ETHEREAL TRANSFERENCE?*
ANYONE? JACOB! PLEASE STEP FORWARD.
I ASK YOU TO PLEASE REMOVE ANY TEN CARDS FROM THE DECK.
OKAY, COACH. I HAVE THEM.
NOW, PLEASE CONCEAL YOUR CHOSEN CARDS AS BEST YOU CAN.
EXCELLENT CHOICE, JACOB. SURELY, I CAN'T GET TO THEM FROM HERE.

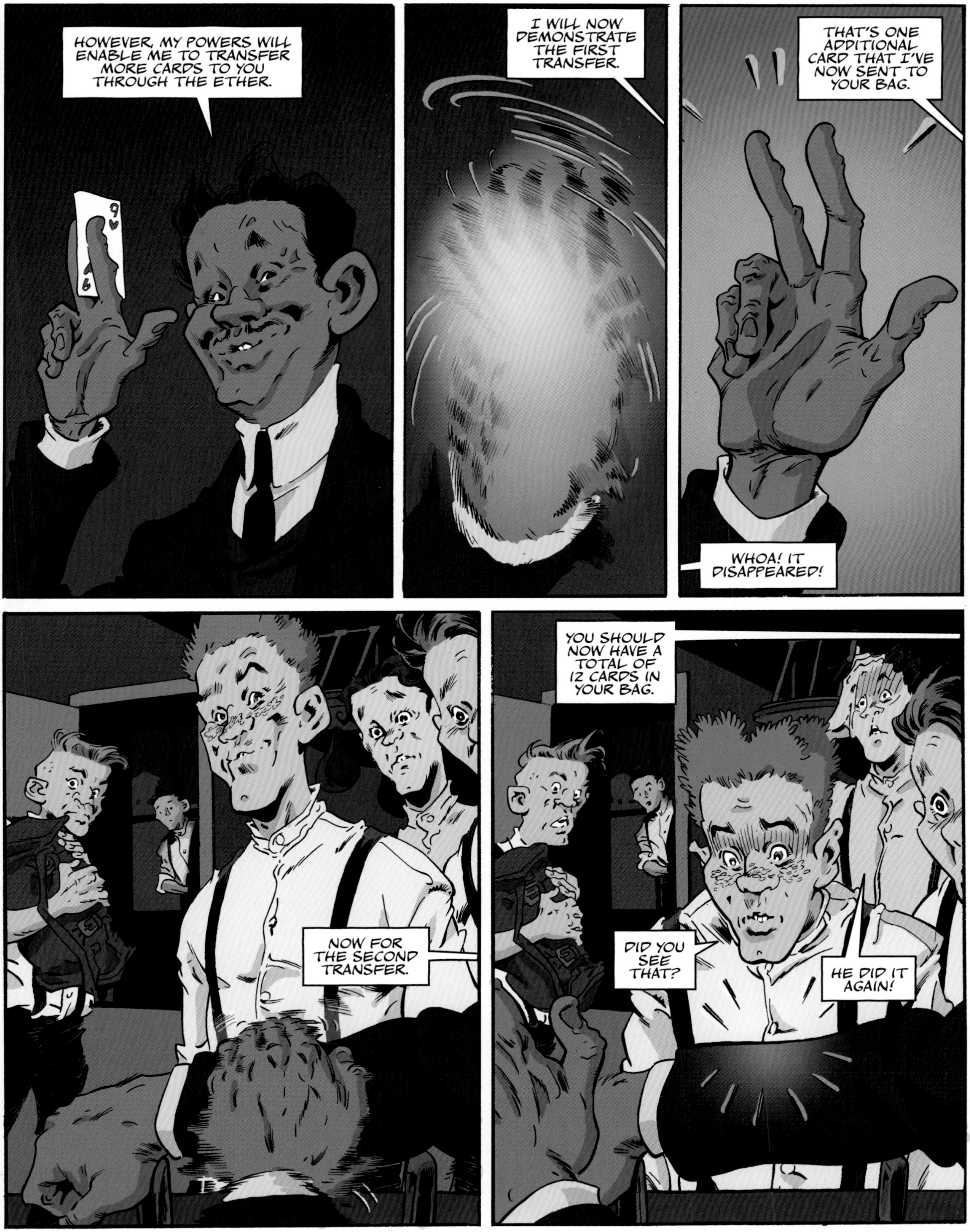
HOWEVER, MY POWERS WILL ENABLE ME TO TRANSFER MORE CARDS TO YOU THROUGH THE ETHER.
I WILL NOW DEMONSTRATE THE FIRST TRANSFER.
THAT'S ONE ADDITIONAL CARD THAT I'VE NOW SENT TO YOUR BAG.
WHOA! IT DISAPPEARED!
NOW FOR THE SECOND TRANSFER.
YOU SHOULD NOW HAVE A TOTAL OF 12 CARDS IN YOUR BAG.
DID YOU SEE THAT?
HE DID IT AGAIN!

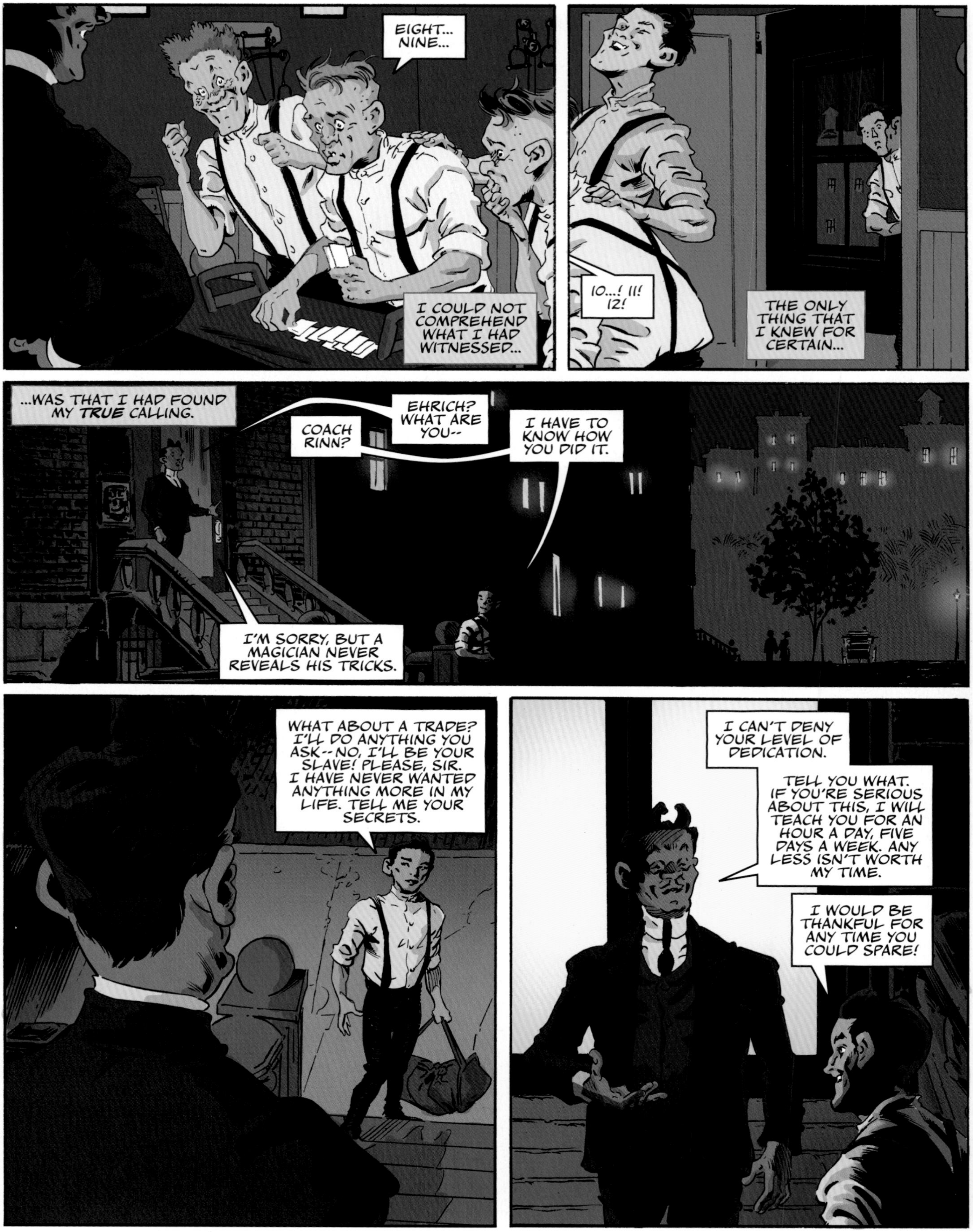
EIGHT... NINE...
I COULD NOT COMPREHEND WHAT I HAD WITNESSED...
10...! 11! 12!
THE ONLY THING THAT I KNEW FOR CERTAIN...
...WAS THAT I HAD FOUND MY TRUE CALLING.
EHRICH? WHAT ARE YOU--
COACH RINN?
I HAVE TO KNOW HOW YOU DID IT.
I'M SORRY, BUT A MAGICIAN NEVER REVEALS HIS TRICKS.
WHAT ABOUT A TRADE? I'LL DO ANYTHING YOU ASK--NO, I'LL BE YOUR SLAVE! PLEASE, SIR. I HAVE NEVER WANTED ANYTHING MORE IN MY LIFE. TELL ME YOUR SECRETS.
I CAN'T DENY YOUR LEVEL OF DEDICATION.
TELL YOU WHAT. IF YOU'RE SERIOUS ABOUT THIS, I WILL TEACH YOU FOR AN HOUR A DAY, FIVE DAYS A WEEK. ANY LESS ISN'T WORTH MY TIME.
I WOULD BE THANKFUL FOR ANY TIME YOU COULD SPARE!

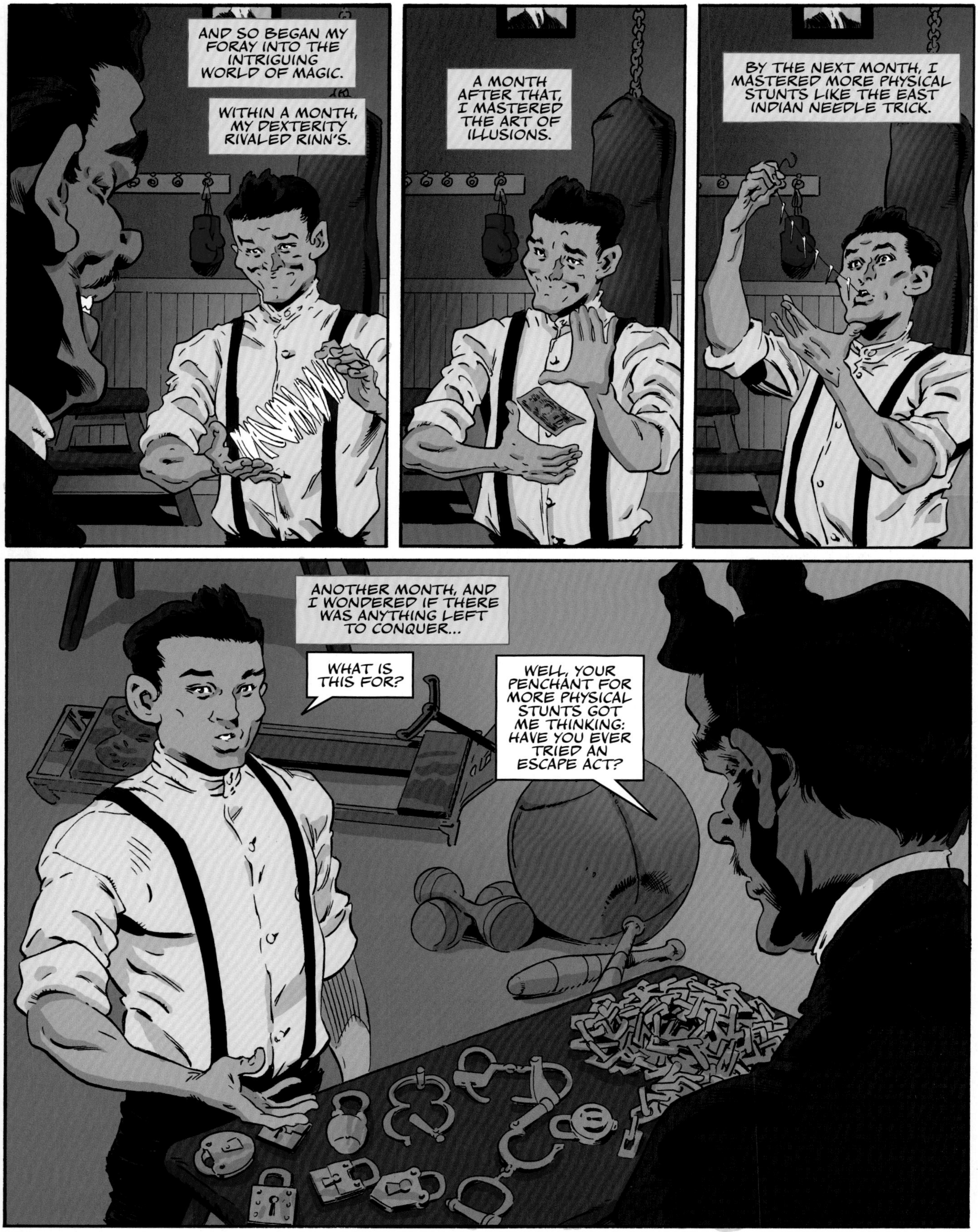
AND SO BEGAN MY FORAY INTO THE INTRIGUING WORLD OF MAGIC.
WITHIN A MONTH, MY DEXTERITY RIVALED RINN'S.
A MONTH AFTER THAT, I MASTERED THE ART OF ILLUSIONS.
BY THE NEXT MONTH, I MASTERED MORE PHYSICAL STUNTS LIKE THE EAST INDIAN NEEDLE TRICK.
ANOTHER MONTH, AND I WONDERED IF THERE WAS ANYTHING LEFT TO CONQUER...
WHAT IS THIS FOR?
WELL, YOUR PENCHANT FOR MORE PHYSICAL STUNTS GOT ME THINKING: HAVE YOU EVER TRIED AN ESCAPE ACT?

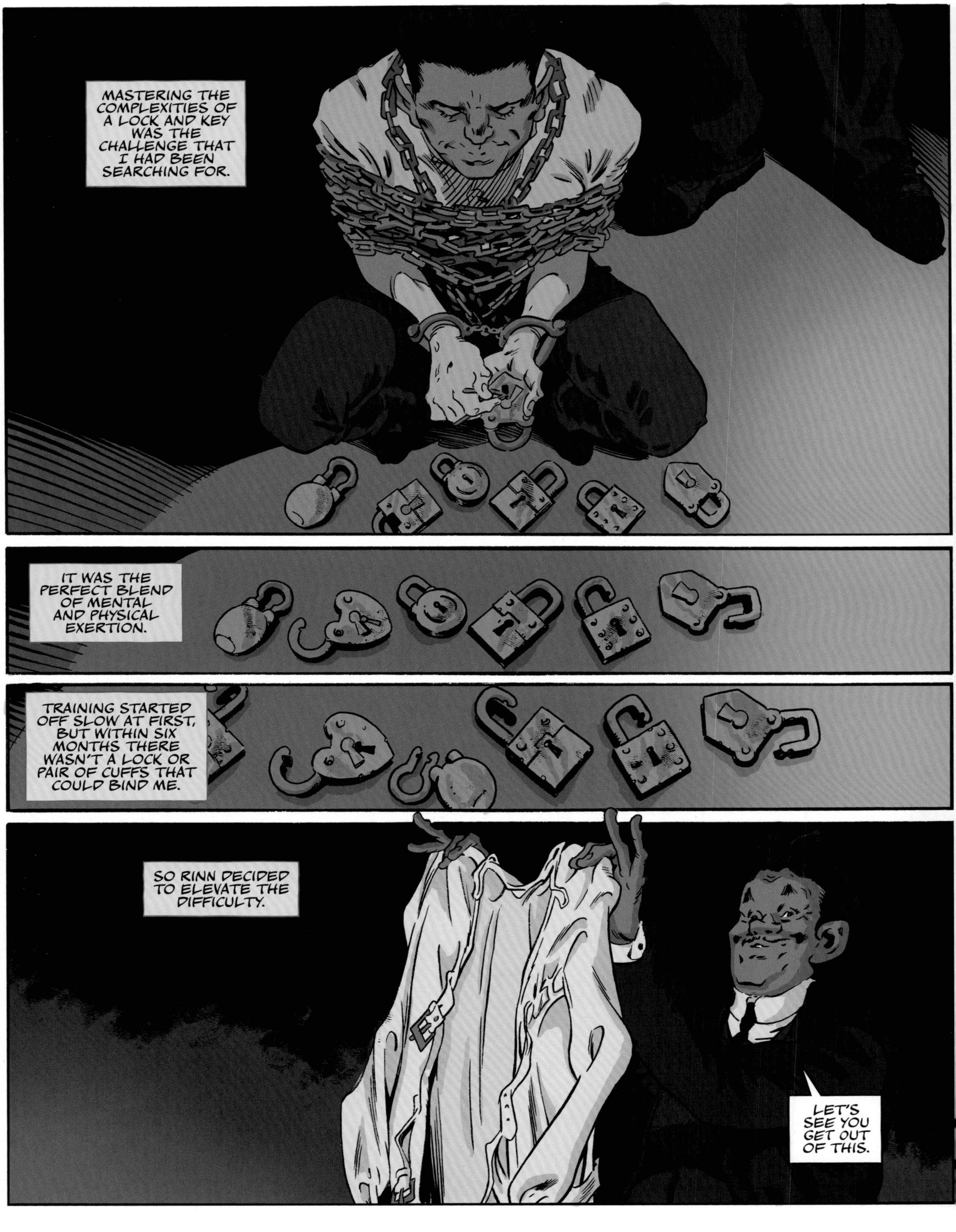

MASTERING THE COMPLEXITIES OF A LOCK AND KEY WAS THE CHALLENGE THAT I HAD BEEN SEARCHING FOR.
IT WAS THE PERFECT BLEND OF MENTAL AND PHYSICAL EXERTION.
TRAINING STARTED OFF SLOW AT FIRST, BUT WITHIN SIX MONTHS THERE WASN'T A LOCK OR PAIR OF CUFFS THAT COULD BIND ME.
SO RINN DECIDED TO ELEVATE THE DIFFICULTY.
LET'S SEE YOU GET OUT OF THIS.

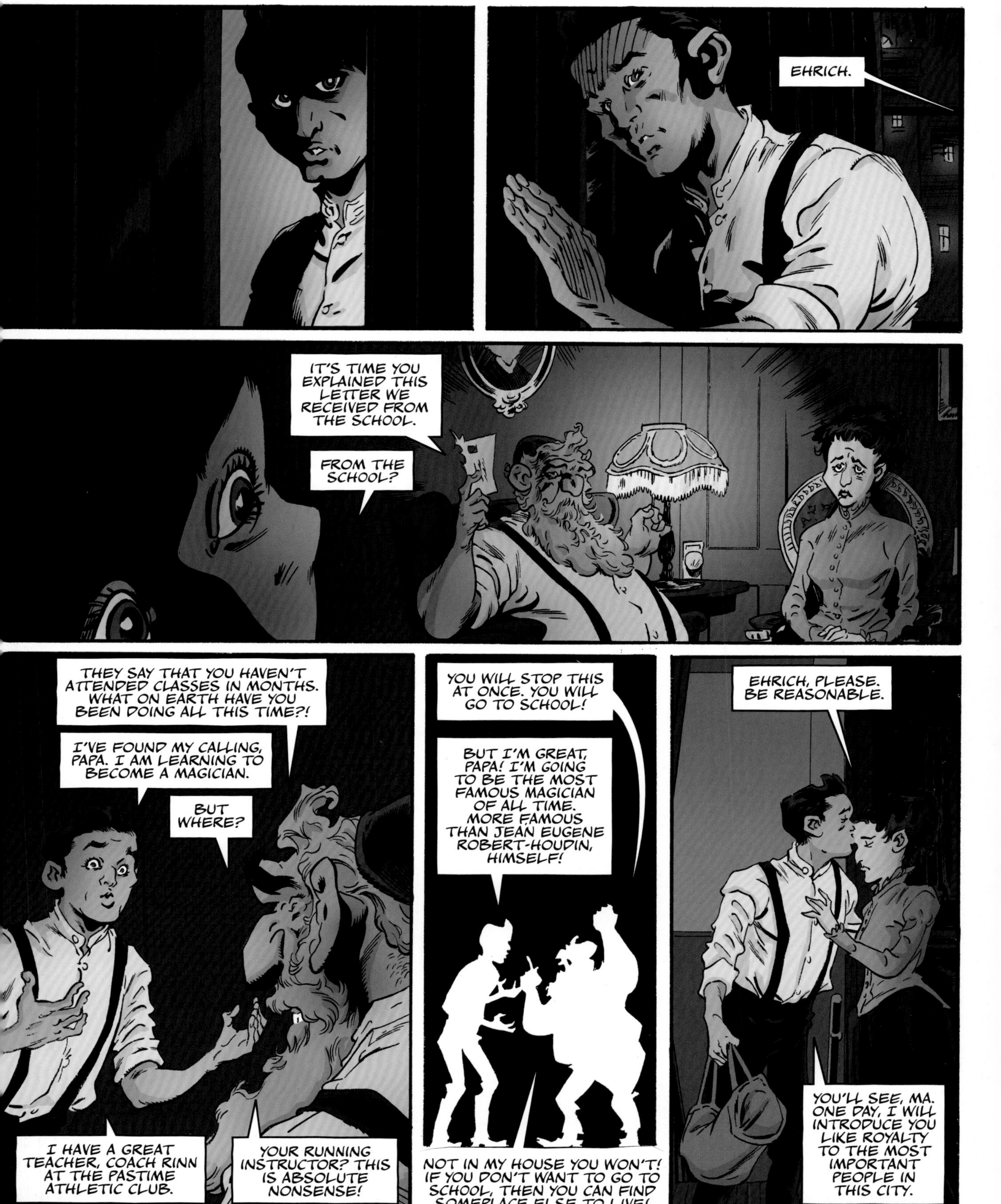
EHRICH.
IT'S TIME YOU EXPLAINED THIS LETTER WE RECEIVED FROM THE SCHOOL.
FROM THE SCHOOL?
THEY SAY THAT YOU HAVEN'T ATTENDED CLASSES IN MONTHS. WHAT ON EARTH HAVE YOU BEEN DOING ALL THIS TIME?!
I'VE FOUND MY CALLING, PAPA. I AM LEARNING TO BECOME A MAGICIAN.
BUT WHERE?
I HAVE A GREAT TEACHER, COACH RINN AT THE PASTIME ATHLETIC CLUB.
YOUR RUNNING INSTRUCTOR? THIS IS ABSOLUTE NONSENSE!
YOU WILL STOP THIS AT ONCE. YOU WILL GO TO SCHOOL!
BUT I'M GREAT, PAPA! I'M GOING TO BE THE MOST FAMOUS MAGICIAN OF ALL TIME. MORE FAMOUS THAN JEAN EUGENE ROBERT-HOUDIN, HIMSELF!
NOT IN MY HOUSE YOU WON'T! IF YOU DON'T WANT TO GO TO SCHOOL, THEN YOU CAN FIND SOMEPLACE ELSE TO LIVE!
EHRICH, PLEASE. BE REASONABLE.
YOU'LL SEE, MA. ONE DAY, I WILL INTRODUCE YOU LIKE ROYALTY TO THE MOST IMPORTANT PEOPLE IN THIS CITY.

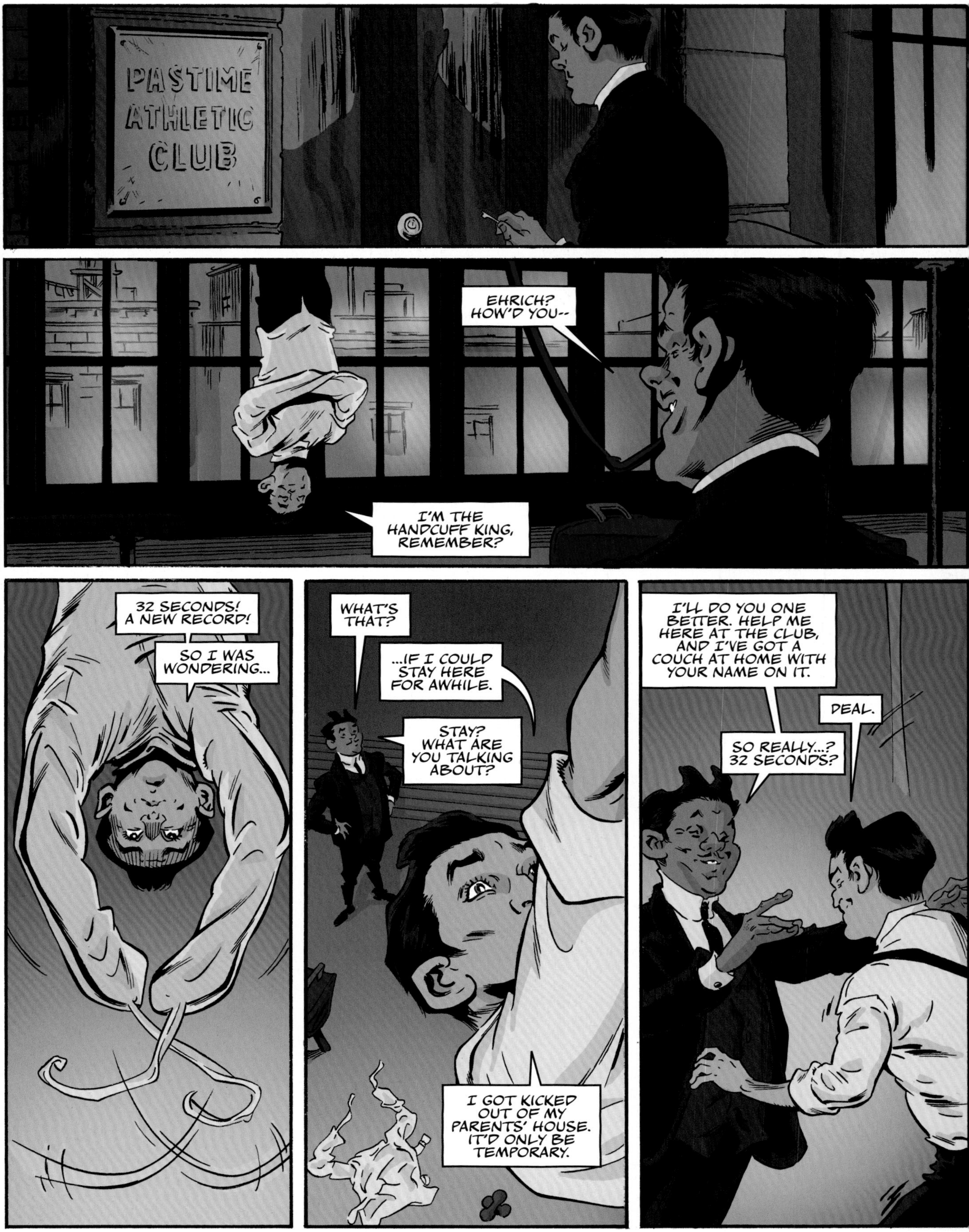
PASTIME ATHLETIC CLUB
EHRICH? HOW'D YOU--
I'M THE HANDCUFF KING, REMEMBER?
32 SECONDS! A NEW RECORD!
SO I WAS WONDERING...
WHAT'S THAT?
...IF I COULD STAY HERE FOR AWHILE.
STAY? WHAT ARE YOU TALKING ABOUT?
I GOT KICKED OUT OF MY PARENTS' HOUSE. IT'D ONLY BE TEMPORARY.
I'LL DO YOU ONE BETTER. HELP ME HERE AT THE CLUB, AND I'VE GOT A COUCH AT HOME WITH YOUR NAME ON IT.
DEAL.
SO REALLY...? 32 SECONDS?

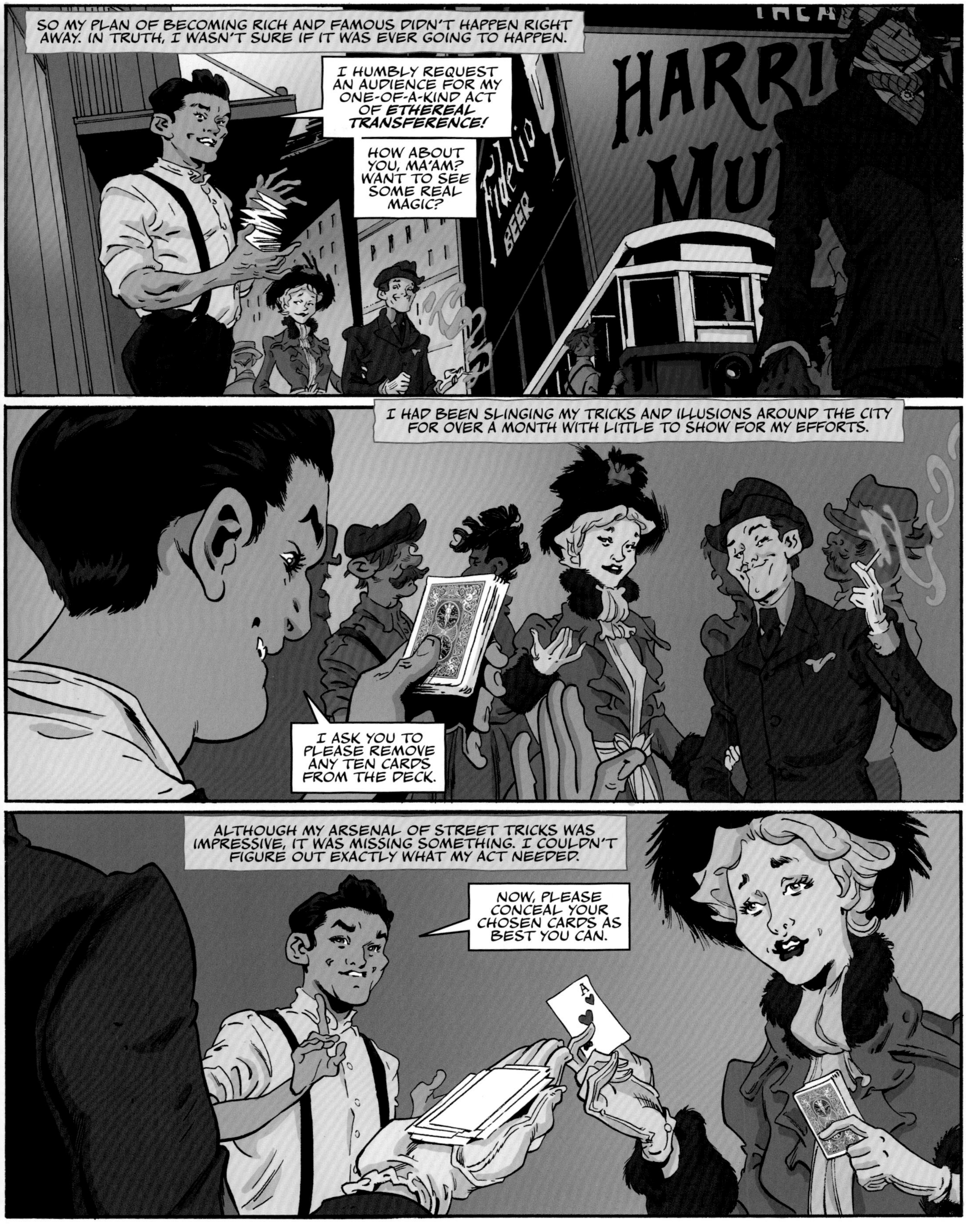
SO MY PLAN OF BECOMING RICH AND FAMOUS DIDN'T HAPPEN RIGHT AWAY. IN TRUTH, I WASN'T SURE IF IT WAS EVER GOING TO HAPPEN.
I HUMBLY REQUEST AN AUDIENCE FOR MY ONE-OF-A-KIND ACT OF ETHEREAL TRANSFERENCE!
HOW ABOUT YOU, MA'AM? WANT TO SEE SOME REAL MAGIC?
HARRI
MU
Fidelio BEER
I HAD BEEN SLINGING MY TRICKS AND ILLUSIONS AROUND THE CITY FOR OVER A MONTH WITH LITTLE TO SHOW FOR MY EFFORTS.
I ASK YOU TO PLEASE REMOVE ANY TEN CARDS FROM THE DECK.
ALTHOUGH MY ARSENAL OF STREET TRICKS WAS IMPRESSIVE, IT WAS MISSING SOMETHING. I COULDN'T FIGURE OUT EXACTLY WHAT MY ACT NEEDED.
NOW, PLEASE CONCEAL YOUR CHOSEN CARDS AS BEST YOU CAN.

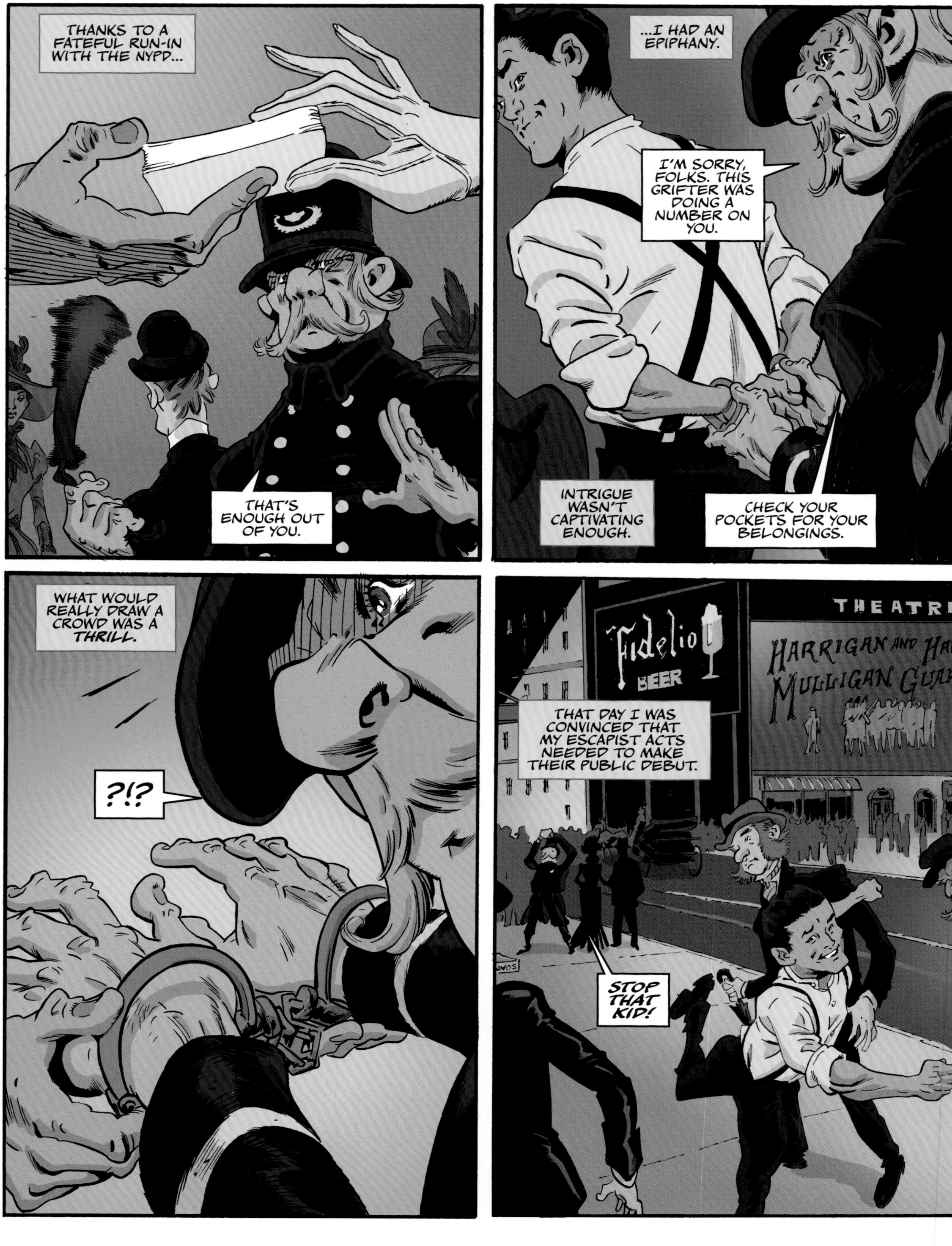
THANKS TO A FATEFUL RUN-IN WITH THE NYPD...
THAT'S ENOUGH OUT OF YOU.
...I HAD AN EPIPHANY.
I'M SORRY, FOLKS. THIS GRIFTER WAS DOING A NUMBER ON YOU.
INTRIGUE WASN'T CAPTIVATING ENOUGH.
CHECK YOUR POCKETS FOR YOUR BELONGINGS.
WHAT WOULD REALLY DRAW A CROWD WAS A *THRILL*.
?!?
THEATRE
Fidelio
BEER
HARRIGAN AND
MULLIGAN
THAT DAY I WAS CONVINCED THAT MY ESCAPIST ACTS NEEDED TO MAKE THEIR PUBLIC DEBUT.
STOP THAT KID!

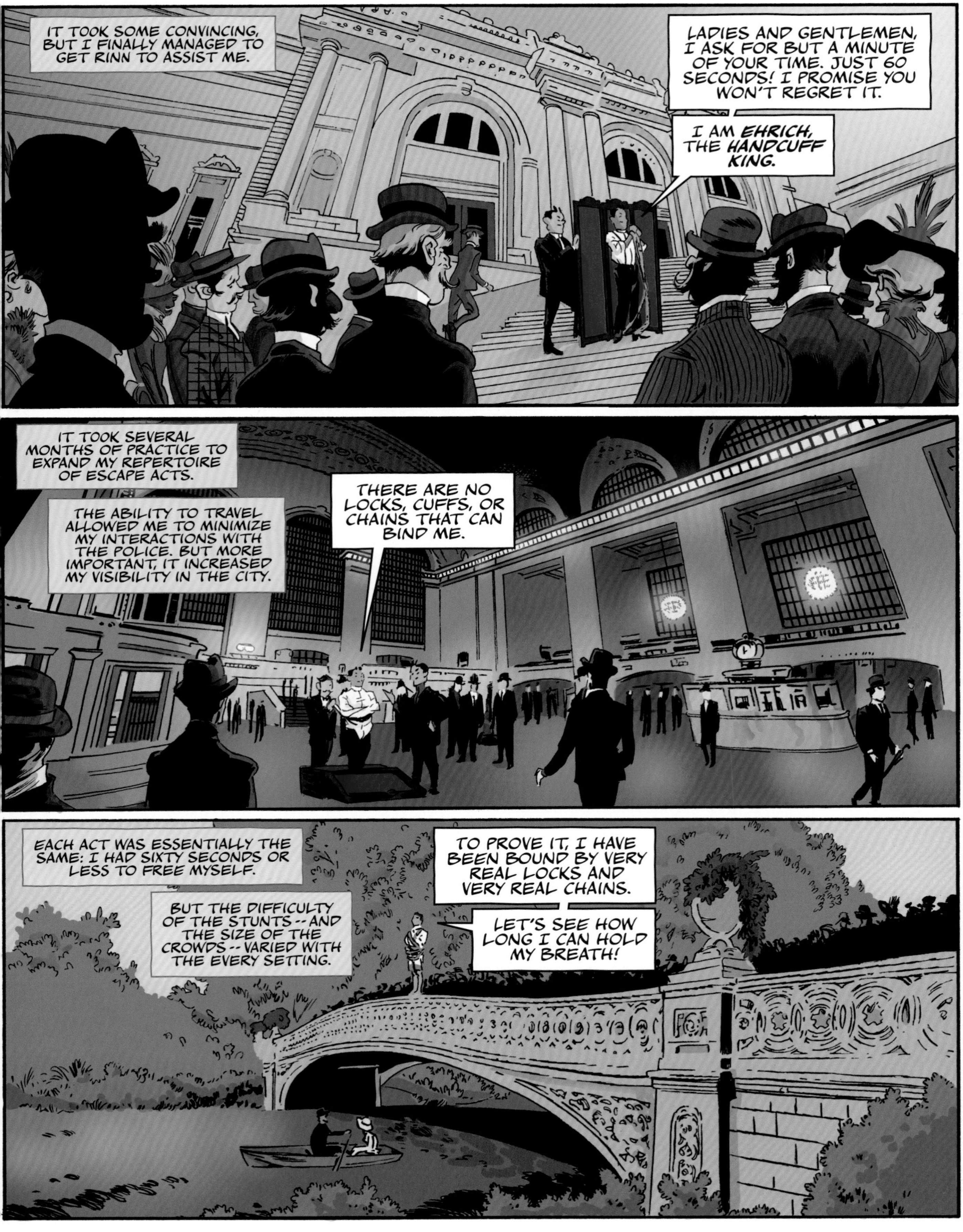
IT TOOK SOME CONVINCING, BUT I FINALLY MANAGED TO GET RINN TO ASSIST ME.
LADIES AND GENTLEMEN, I ASK FOR BUT A MINUTE OF YOUR TIME. JUST 60 SECONDS! I PROMISE YOU WON'T REGRET IT.
I AM *EHRICH*, THE *HANDCUFF KING*.
IT TOOK SEVERAL MONTHS OF PRACTICE TO EXPAND MY REPERTOIRE OF ESCAPE ACTS.
THE ABILITY TO TRAVEL ALLOWED ME TO MINIMIZE MY INTERACTIONS WITH THE POLICE. BUT MORE IMPORTANT, IT INCREASED MY VISIBILITY IN THE CITY.
THERE ARE NO LOCKS, CUFFS, OR CHAINS THAT CAN BIND ME.
EACH ACT WAS ESSENTIALLY THE SAME: I HAD SIXTY SECONDS OR LESS TO FREE MYSELF.
BUT THE DIFFICULTY OF THE STUNTS -- AND THE SIZE OF THE CROWDS -- VARIED WITH THE EVERY SETTING.
TO PROVE IT, I HAVE BEEN BOUND BY VERY REAL LOCKS AND VERY REAL CHAINS.
LET'S SEE HOW LONG I CAN HOLD MY BREATH!

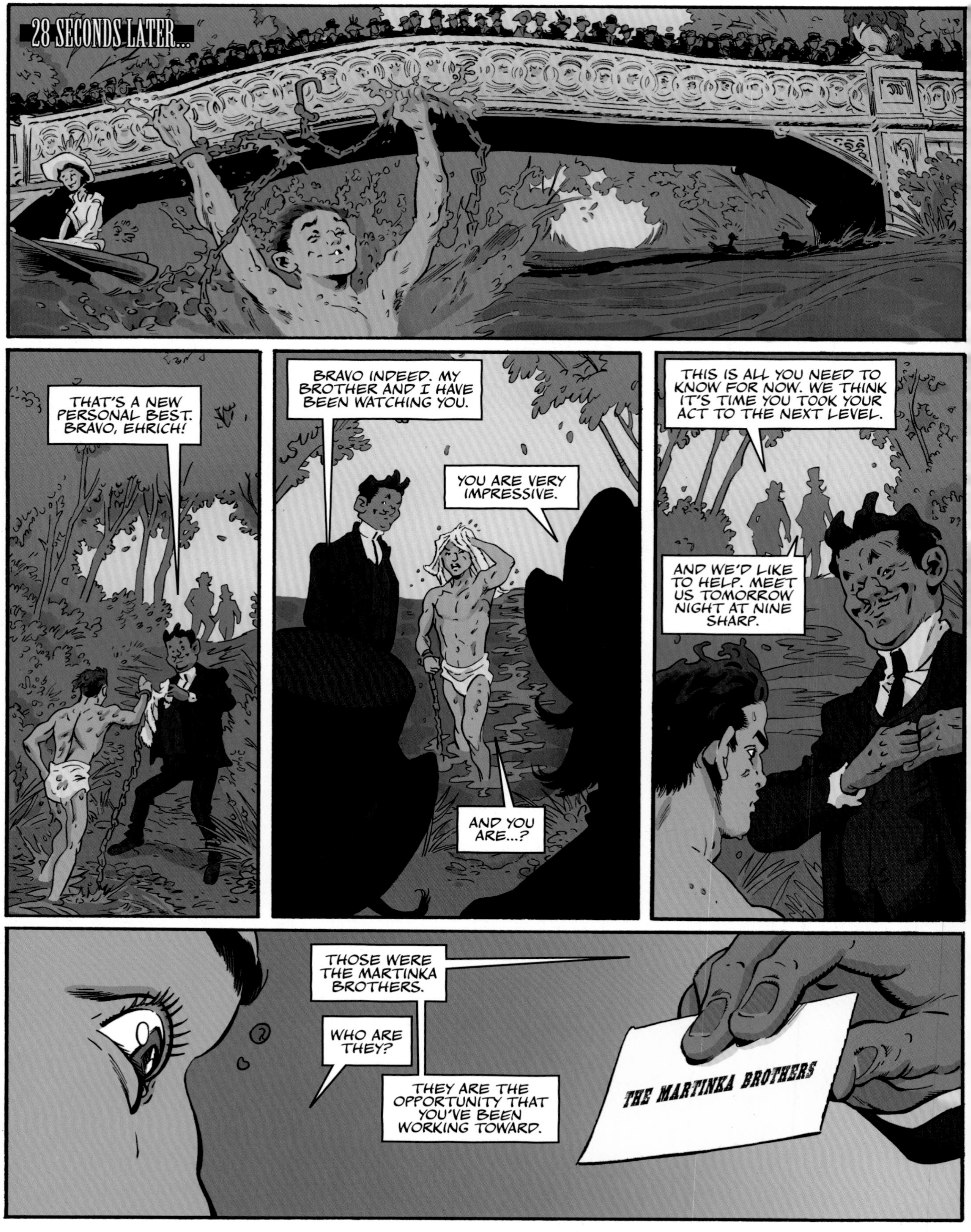
28 SECONDS LATER...
THAT'S A NEW PERSONAL BEST. BRAVO, EHRICH!
BRAVO INDEED. MY BROTHER AND I HAVE BEEN WATCHING YOU.
YOU ARE VERY IMPRESSIVE.
AND YOU ARE...?
THIS IS ALL YOU NEED TO KNOW FOR NOW. WE THINK IT'S TIME YOU TOOK YOUR ACT TO THE NEXT LEVEL.
AND WE'D LIKE TO HELP. MEET US TOMORROW NIGHT AT NINE SHARP.
THOSE WERE THE MARTINKA BROTHERS.
WHO ARE THEY?
THEY ARE THE OPPORTUNITY THAT YOU'VE BEEN WORKING TOWARD.
THE MARTINKA BROTHERS

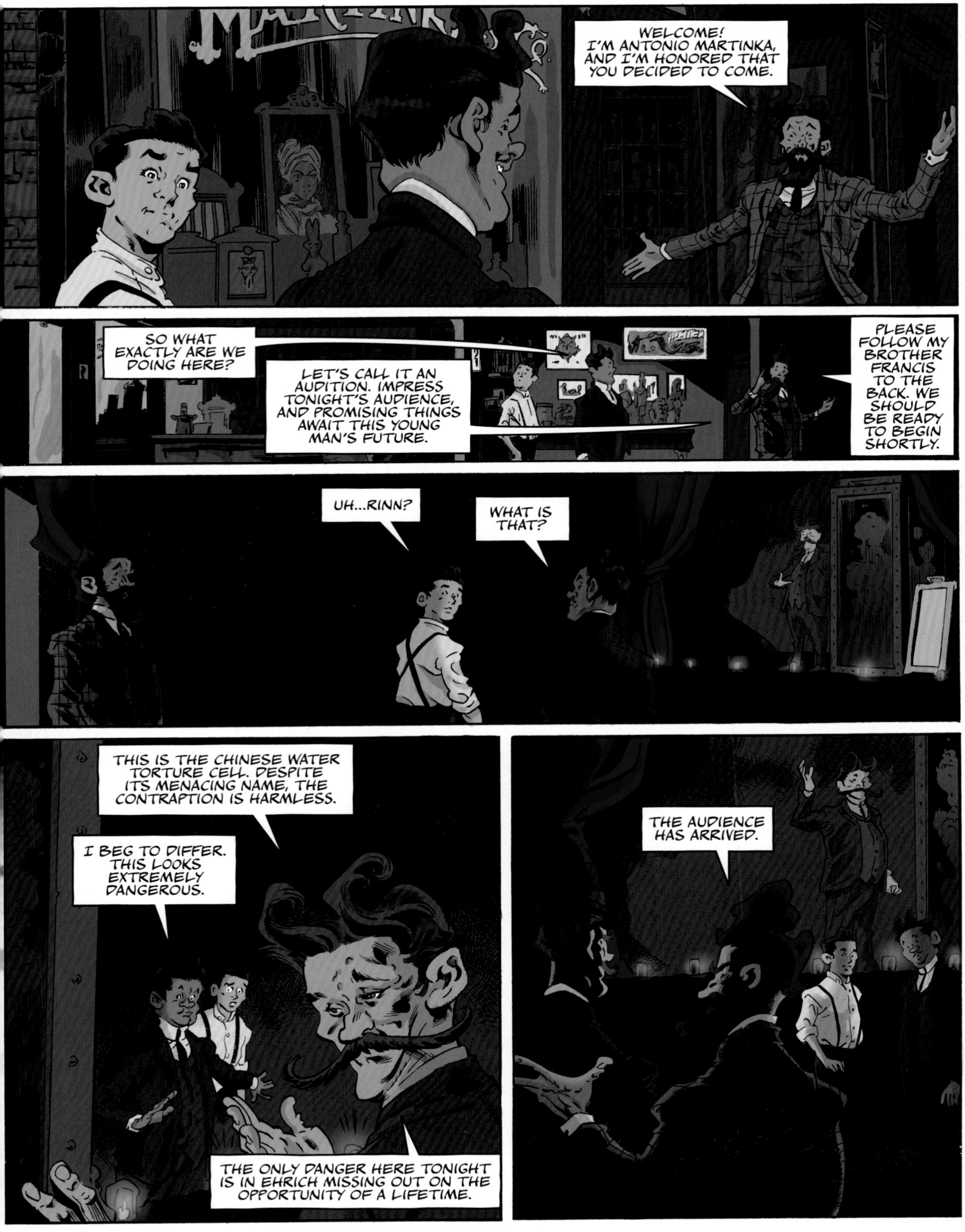
WELCOME! I'M ANTONIO MARTINKA, AND I'M HONORED THAT YOU DECIDED TO COME.
SO WHAT EXACTLY ARE WE DOING HERE?
LET'S CALL IT AN AUDITION. IMPRESS TONIGHT'S AUDIENCE, AND PROMISING THINGS AWAIT THIS YOUNG MAN'S FUTURE.
PLEASE FOLLOW MY BROTHER FRANCIS TO THE BACK. WE SHOULD BE READY TO BEGIN SHORTLY.
UH...RINN?
WHAT IS THAT?
THIS IS THE CHINESE WATER TORTURE CELL. DESPITE ITS MENACING NAME, THE CONTRAPTION IS HARMLESS.
I BEG TO DIFFER. THIS LOOKS EXTREMELY DANGEROUS.
THE ONLY DANGER HERE TONIGHT IS IN EHRICH MISSING OUT ON THE OPPORTUNITY OF A LIFETIME.
THE AUDIENCE HAS ARRIVED.

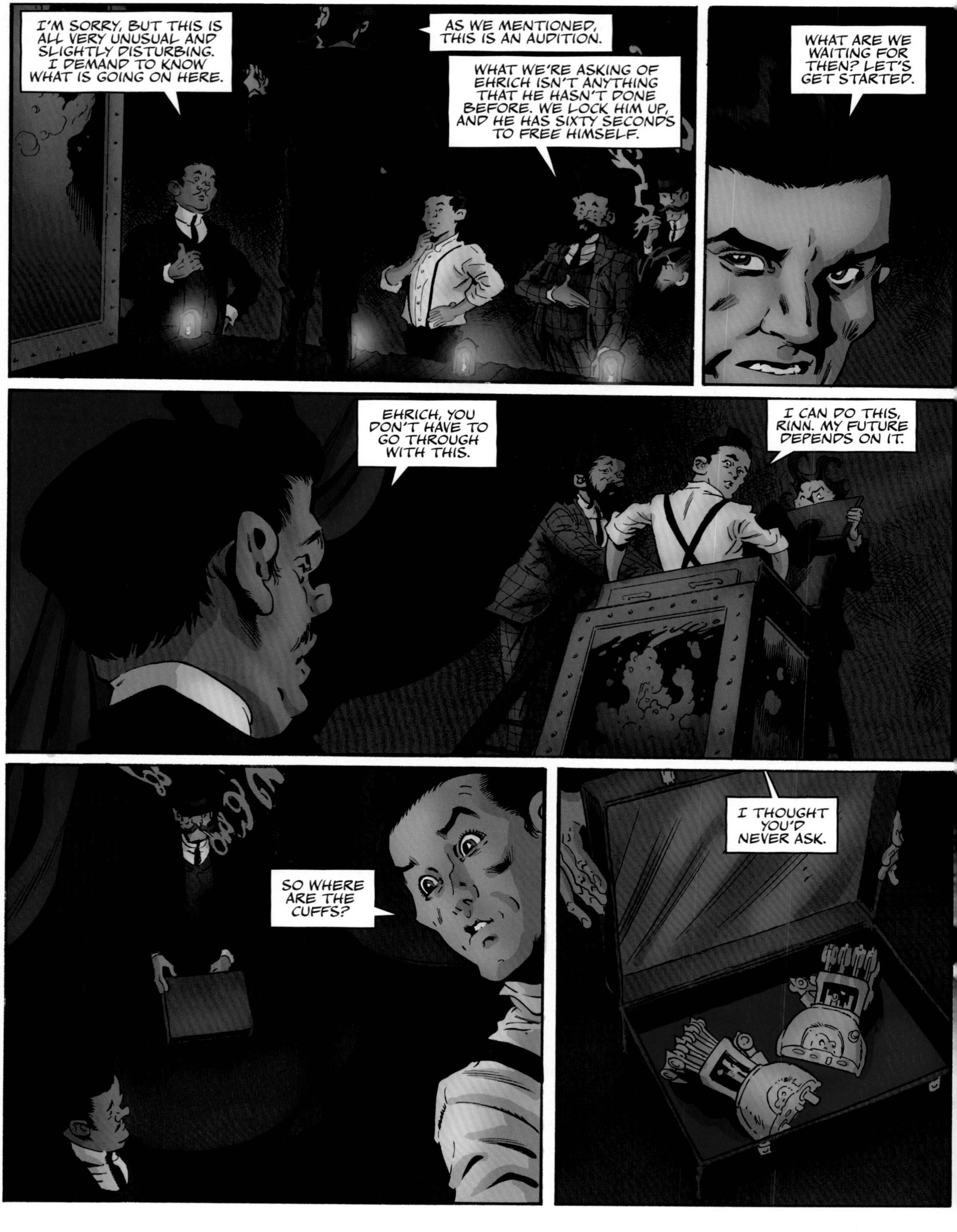
I'M SORRY, BUT THIS IS ALL VERY UNUSUAL AND SLIGHTLY DISTURBING. I DEMAND TO KNOW WHAT IS GOING ON HERE.
AS WE MENTIONED, THIS IS AN AUDITION.
WHAT WE'RE ASKING OF EHRICH ISN'T ANYTHING THAT HE HASN'T DONE BEFORE. WE LOCK HIM UP, AND HE HAS SIXTY SECONDS TO FREE HIMSELF.
WHAT ARE WE WAITING FOR THEN? LET'S GET STARTED.
EHRICH, YOU DON'T HAVE TO GO THROUGH WITH THIS.
I CAN DO THIS, RINN. MY FUTURE DEPENDS ON IT.
SO WHERE ARE THE CUFFS?
I THOUGHT YOU'D NEVER ASK.

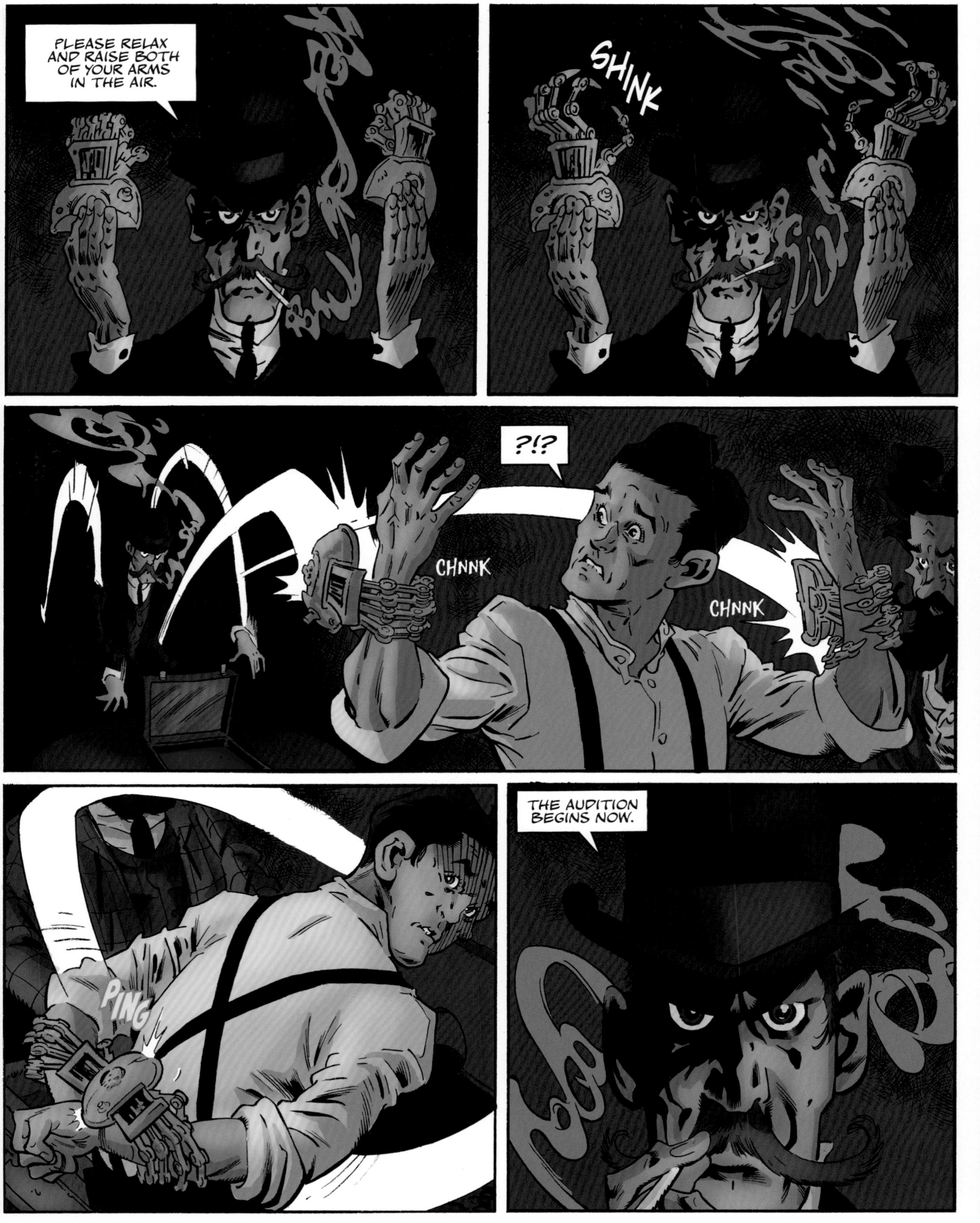
PLEASE RELAX AND RAISE BOTH OF YOUR ARMS IN THE AIR.
SHINK
?!?
CHNNK
CHNNK
PING
THE AUDITION BEGINS NOW.

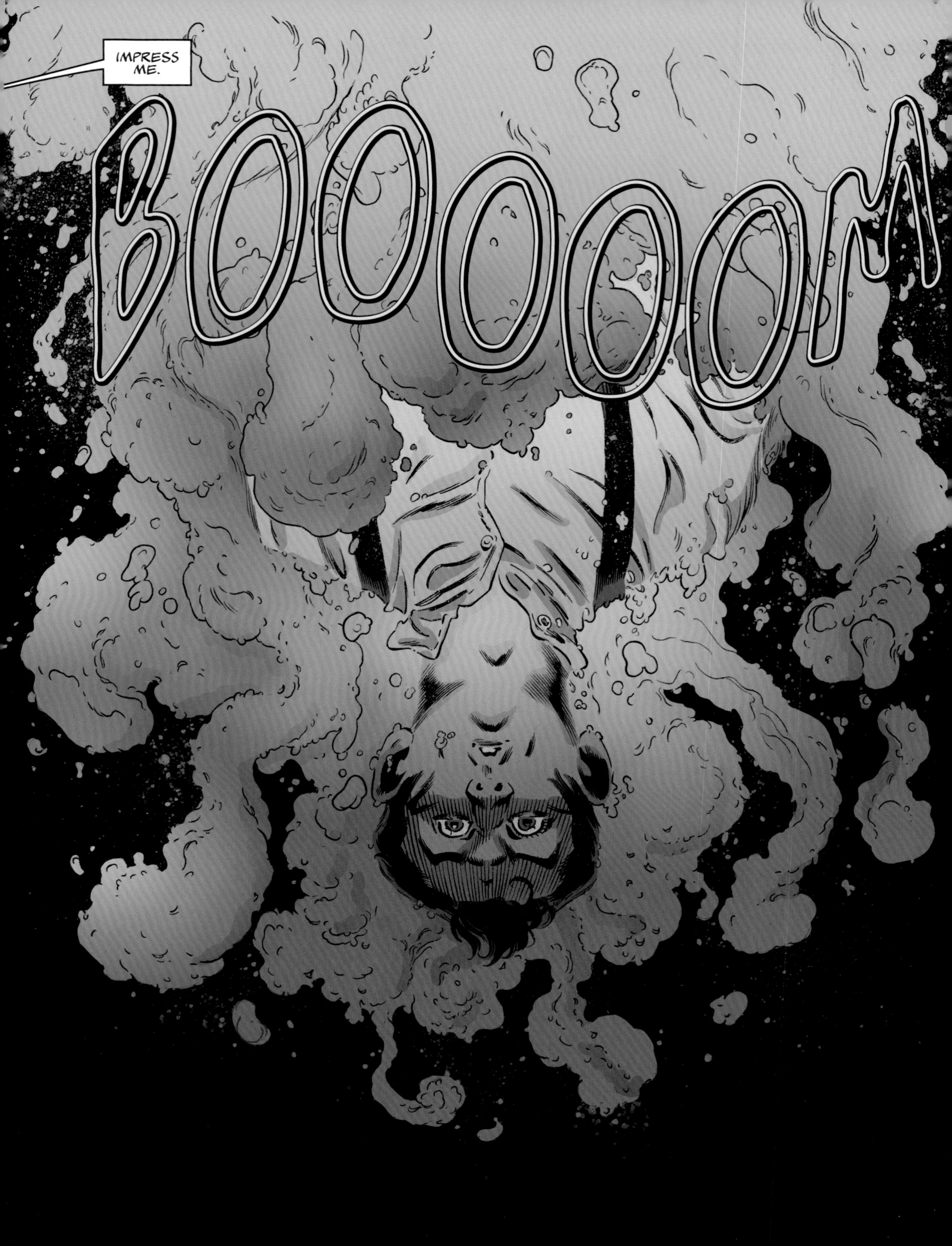
IMPRESS ME.
BOOOOOM

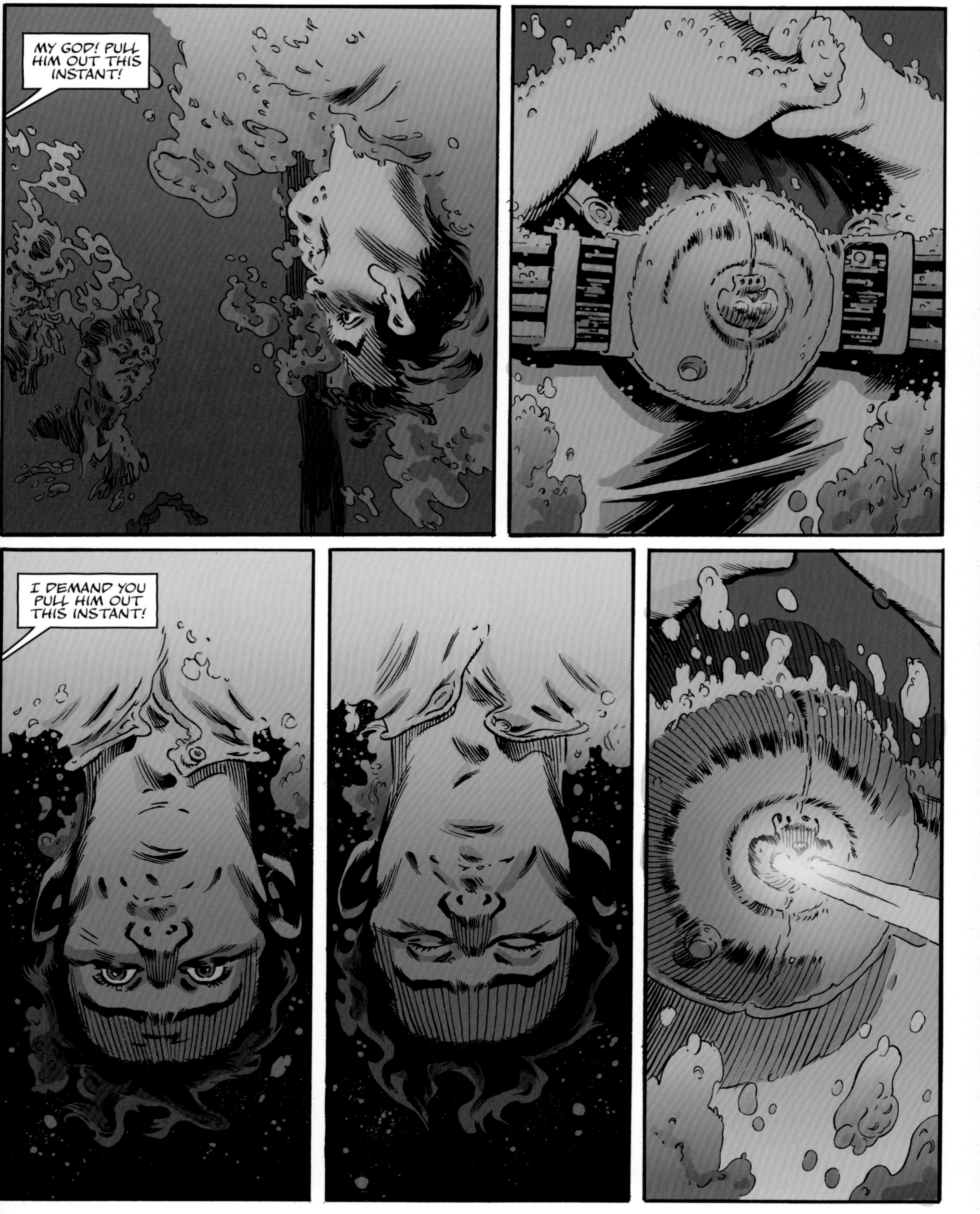
MY GOD! PULL HIM OUT THIS INSTANT!
I DEMAND YOU PULL HIM OUT THIS INSTANT!

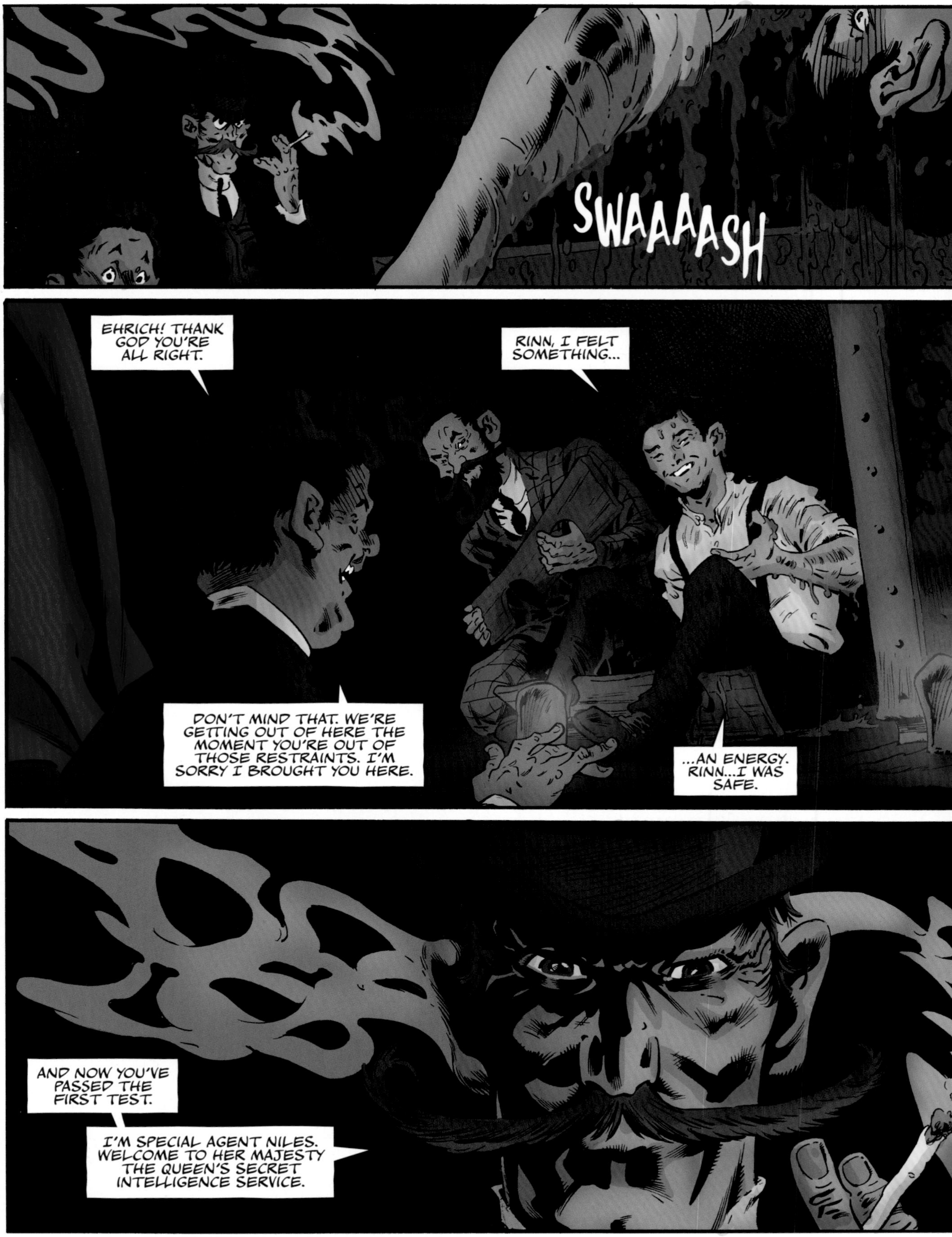
SWAAAASH
EHRICH! THANK GOD YOU'RE ALL RIGHT.
RINN, I FELT SOMETHING...
DON'T MIND THAT. WE'RE GETTING OUT OF HERE THE MOMENT YOU'RE OUT OF THOSE RESTRAINTS. I'M SORRY I BROUGHT YOU HERE.
...AN ENERGY. RINN...I WAS SAFE.
AND NOW YOU'VE PASSED THE FIRST TEST.
I'M SPECIAL AGENT NILES. WELCOME TO HER MAJESTY THE QUEEN'S SECRET INTELLIGENCE SERVICE.

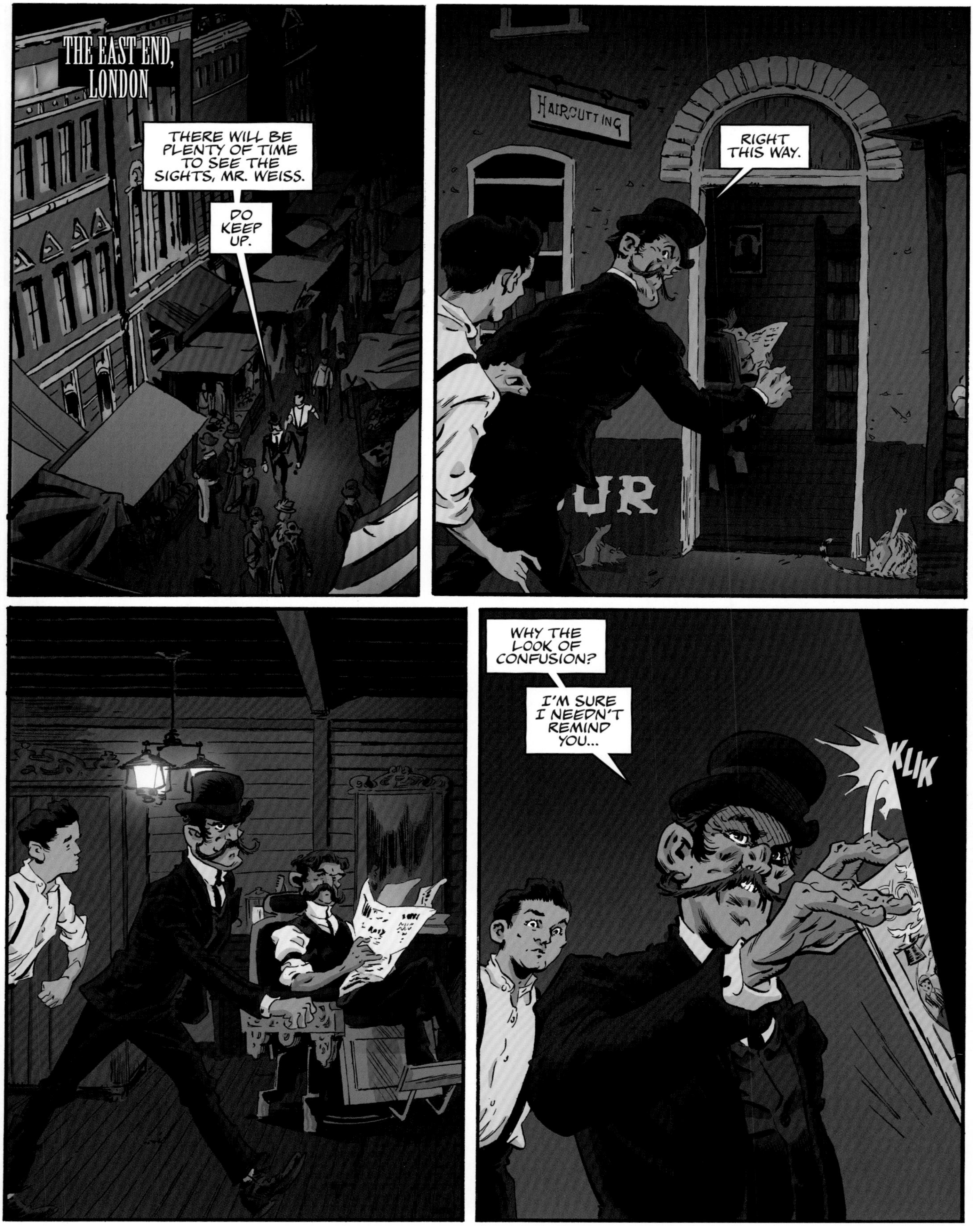

THE EAST END, LONDON
THERE WILL BE PLENTY OF TIME TO SEE THE SIGHTS, MR. WEISS.
DO KEEP UP.
HAIRCUTTING
RIGHT THIS WAY.
WHY THE LOOK OF CONFUSION?
I'M SURE I NEEDN'T REMIND YOU...
KLIK

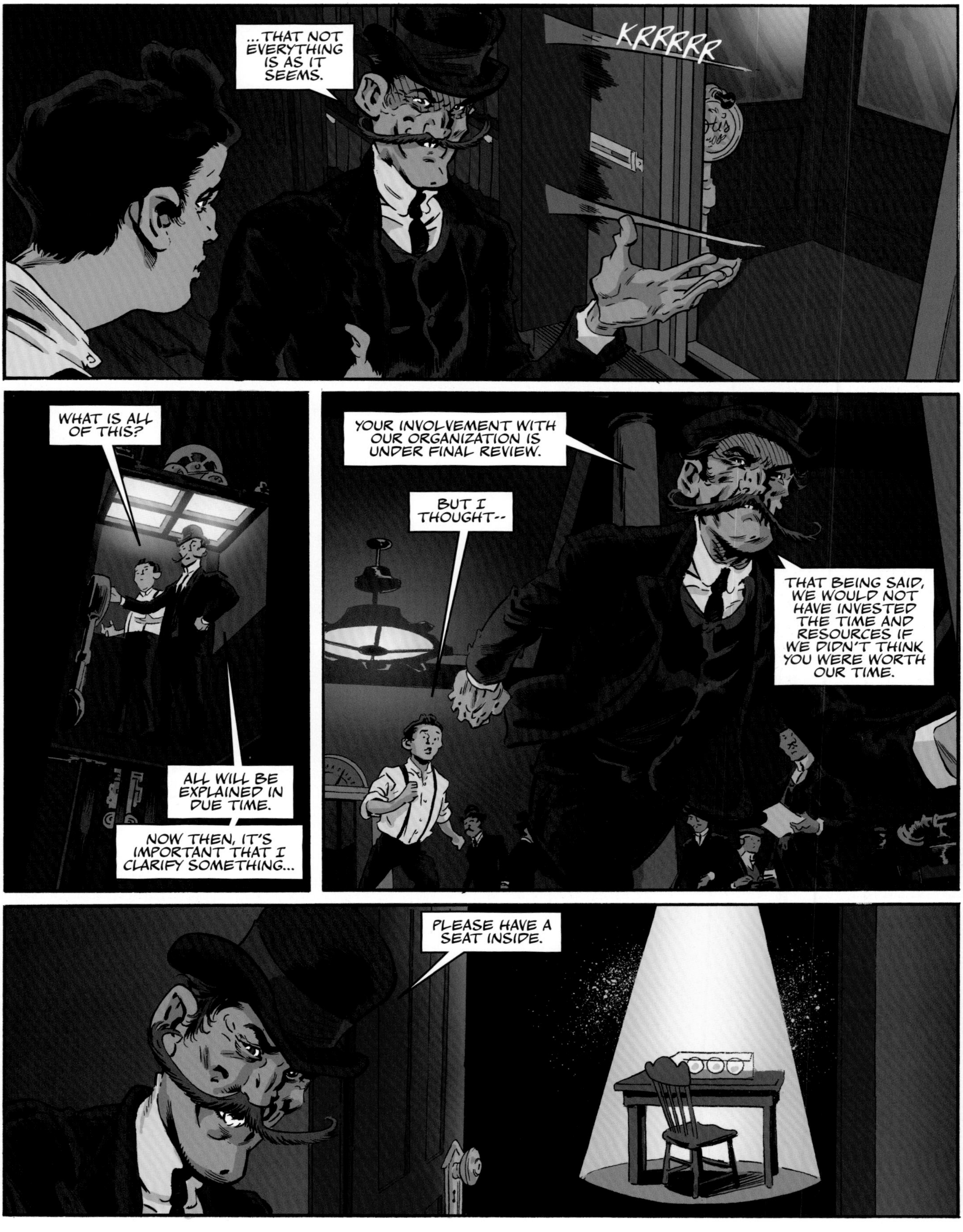
...THAT NOT EVERYTHING IS AS IT SEEMS.
KRRRRR
WHAT IS ALL OF THIS?
ALL WILL BE EXPLAINED IN DUE TIME.
NOW THEN, IT'S IMPORTANT THAT I CLARIFY SOMETHING...
YOUR INVOLVEMENT WITH OUR ORGANIZATION IS UNDER FINAL REVIEW.
BUT I THOUGHT--
THAT BEING SAID, WE WOULD NOT HAVE INVESTED THE TIME AND RESOURCES IF WE DIDN'T THINK YOU WERE WORTH OUR TIME.
PLEASE HAVE A SEAT INSIDE.

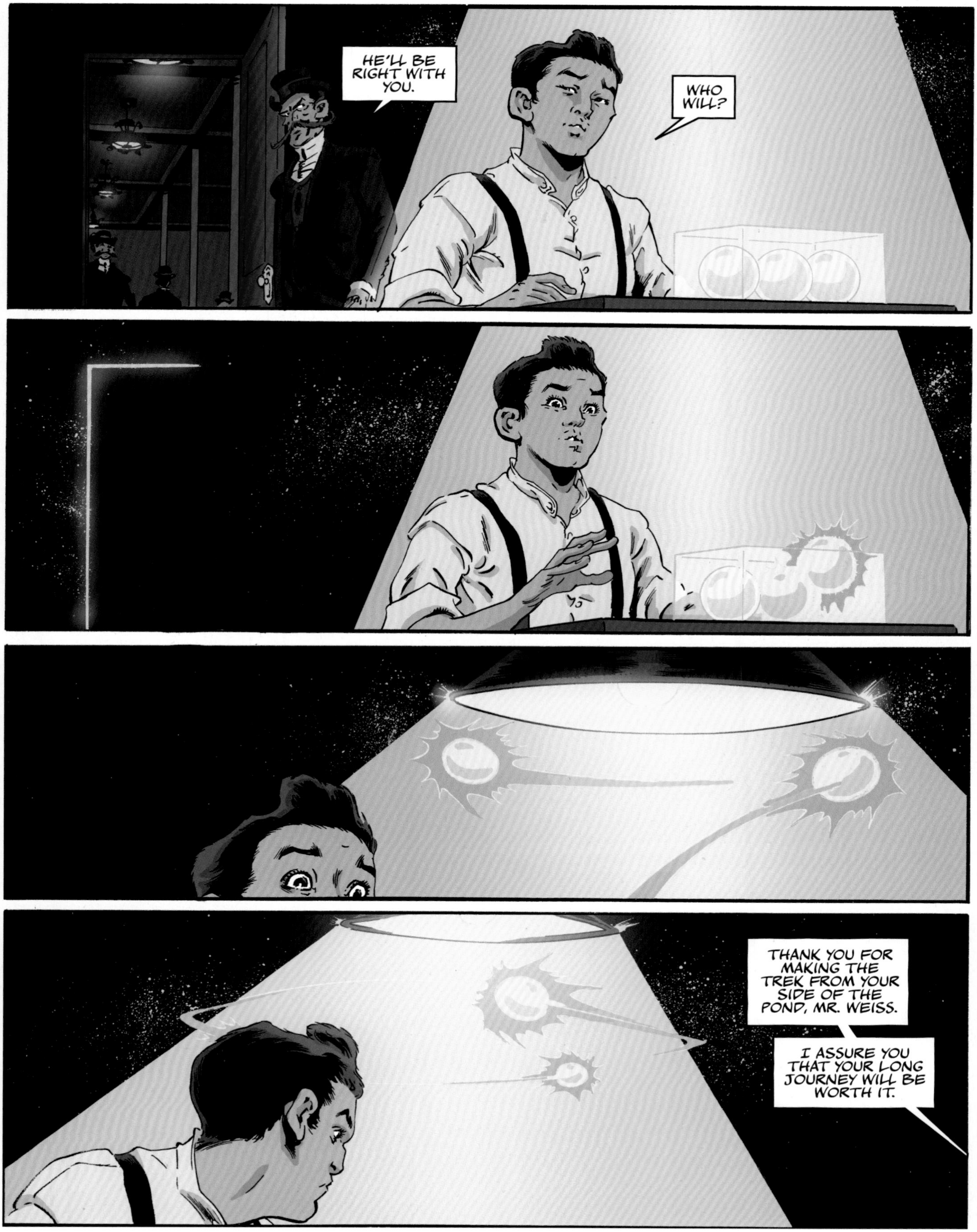
HE'LL BE RIGHT WITH YOU.
WHO WILL?
THANK YOU FOR MAKING THE TREK FROM YOUR SIDE OF THE POND, MR. WEISS.
I ASSURE YOU THAT YOUR LONG JOURNEY WILL BE WORTH IT.

YOU'VE MET MY COLLEAGUE, SPECIAL AGENT NILES, SO YOU KNOW WHO WE ARE. BUT I'M SURE YOU HAVE MORE QUESTIONS...

SO WHY DON'T I START ANSWERING SOME OF THEM FOR YOU.

I AM SPECIAL AGENT MERRICK. I HAVE BEEN TASKED WITH DETERMINING IF YOU CAN AIDE US IN COMBATING AN ENEMY THE LIKES OF WHICH HAVE NEVER BEEN SEEN.

YOU WANT ME TO FIGHT... IN A WAR?

I WISH IT WERE THAT STRAIGHTFORWARD. NO, OUR AFFAIRS REQUIRE A MUCH MORE DELICATE TOUCH. DONE WELL, AND NO ONE WILL EVEN KNOW OF YOUR INVOLVEMENT. WE'LL COMPENSATE YOU HANDSOMELY FOR IT.

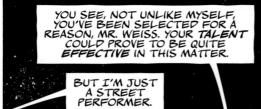

YOU SEE, NOT UNLIKE MYSELF, YOU'VE BEEN SELECTED FOR A REASON, MR. WEISS. YOUR *TALENT* COULD PROVE TO BE QUITE *EFFECTIVE* IN THIS MATTER.

BUT I'M JUST A STREET PERFORMER.

WE BOTH KNOW YOU DON'T BELIEVE THAT.

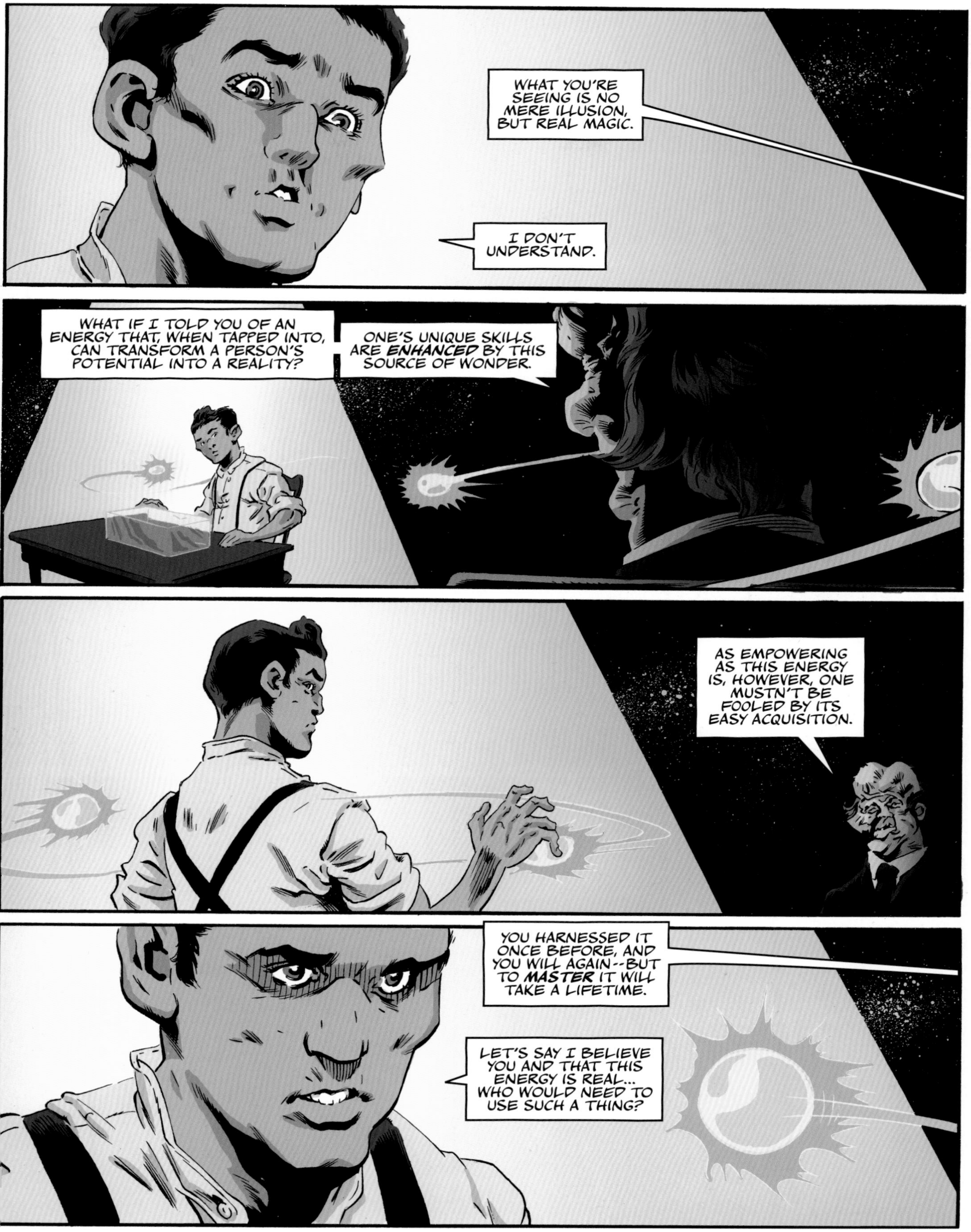
WHAT YOU'RE SEEING IS NO MERE ILLUSION, BUT REAL MAGIC.
I DON'T UNDERSTAND.
WHAT IF I TOLD YOU OF AN ENERGY THAT, WHEN TAPPED INTO, CAN TRANSFORM A PERSON'S POTENTIAL INTO A REALITY?
ONE'S UNIQUE SKILLS ARE ENHANCED BY THIS SOURCE OF WONDER.
AS EMPOWERING AS THIS ENERGY IS, HOWEVER, ONE MUSTN'T BE FOOLED BY ITS EASY ACQUISITION.
YOU HARNESSED IT ONCE BEFORE, AND YOU WILL AGAIN--BUT TO MASTER IT WILL TAKE A LIFETIME.
LET'S SAY I BELIEVE YOU AND THAT THIS ENERGY IS REAL... WHO WOULD NEED TO USE SUCH A THING?

THE ONES WHO FIGHT TO HARNESS IT FOR EVIL GAINS.

IT'S ONLY NATURAL THAT A POSITIVE FORCE BE MET BY A NEGATIVE ONE.

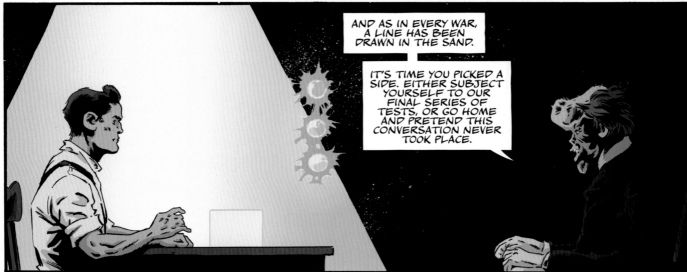

AND AS IN EVERY WAR, A LINE HAS BEEN DRAWN IN THE SAND.

IT'S TIME YOU PICKED A SIDE. EITHER SUBJECT YOURSELF TO OUR FINAL SERIES OF TESTS, OR GO HOME AND PRETEND THIS CONVERSATION NEVER TOOK PLACE.

WHAT KIND OF TESTS?

GRUELING ONES, BOTH MENTALLY AND PHYSICALLY. THEY'VE BEEN TAILORED TO YOU AND WILL DETERMINE YOUR COMPATIBILITY WITH THE ENERGY.

...

WHEN DO WE START?

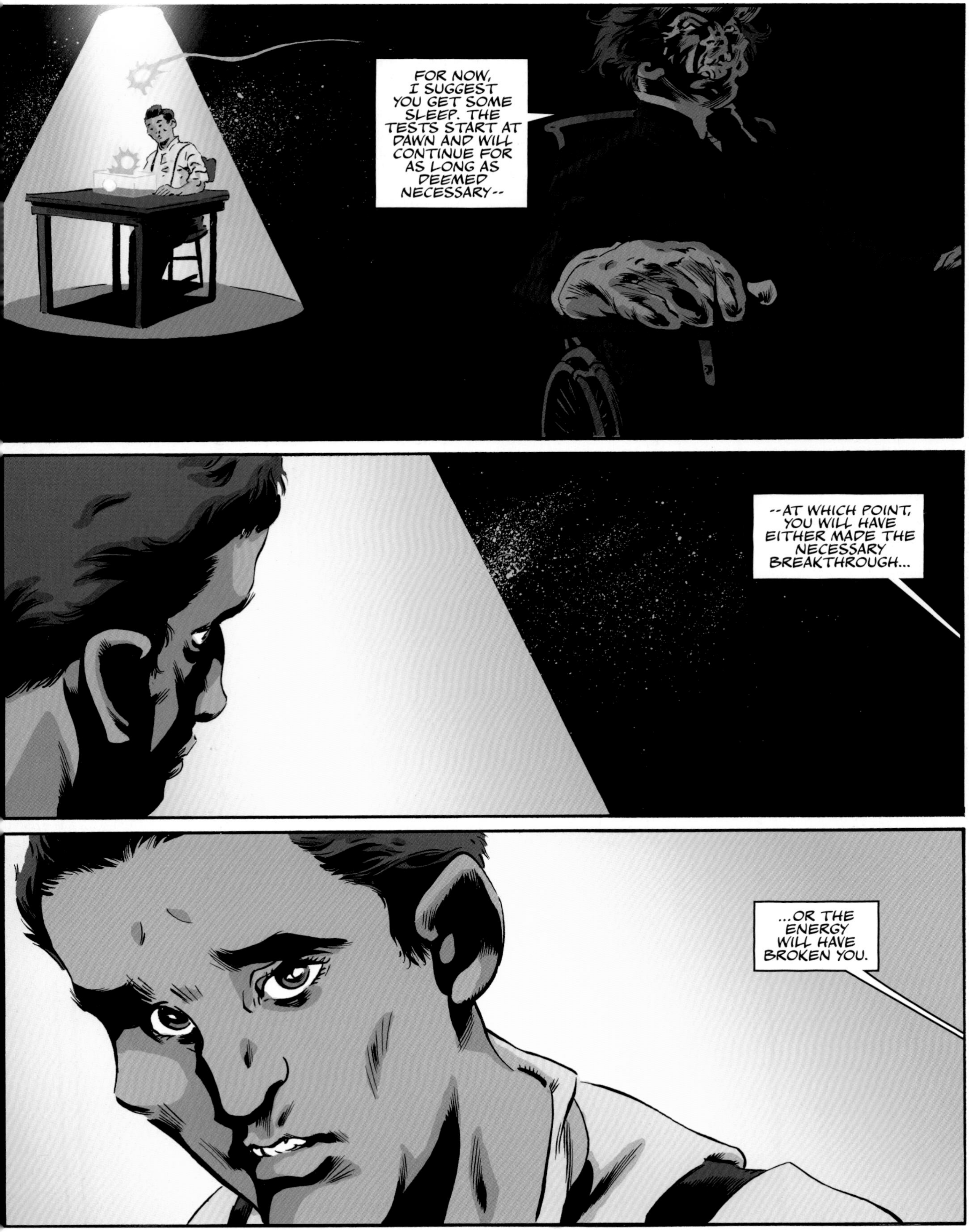
FOR NOW, I SUGGEST YOU GET SOME SLEEP. THE TESTS START AT DAWN AND WILL CONTINUE FOR AS LONG AS DEEMED NECESSARY--
--AT WHICH POINT, YOU WILL HAVE EITHER MADE THE NECESSARY BREAKTHROUGH...
...OR THE ENERGY WILL HAVE BROKEN YOU.

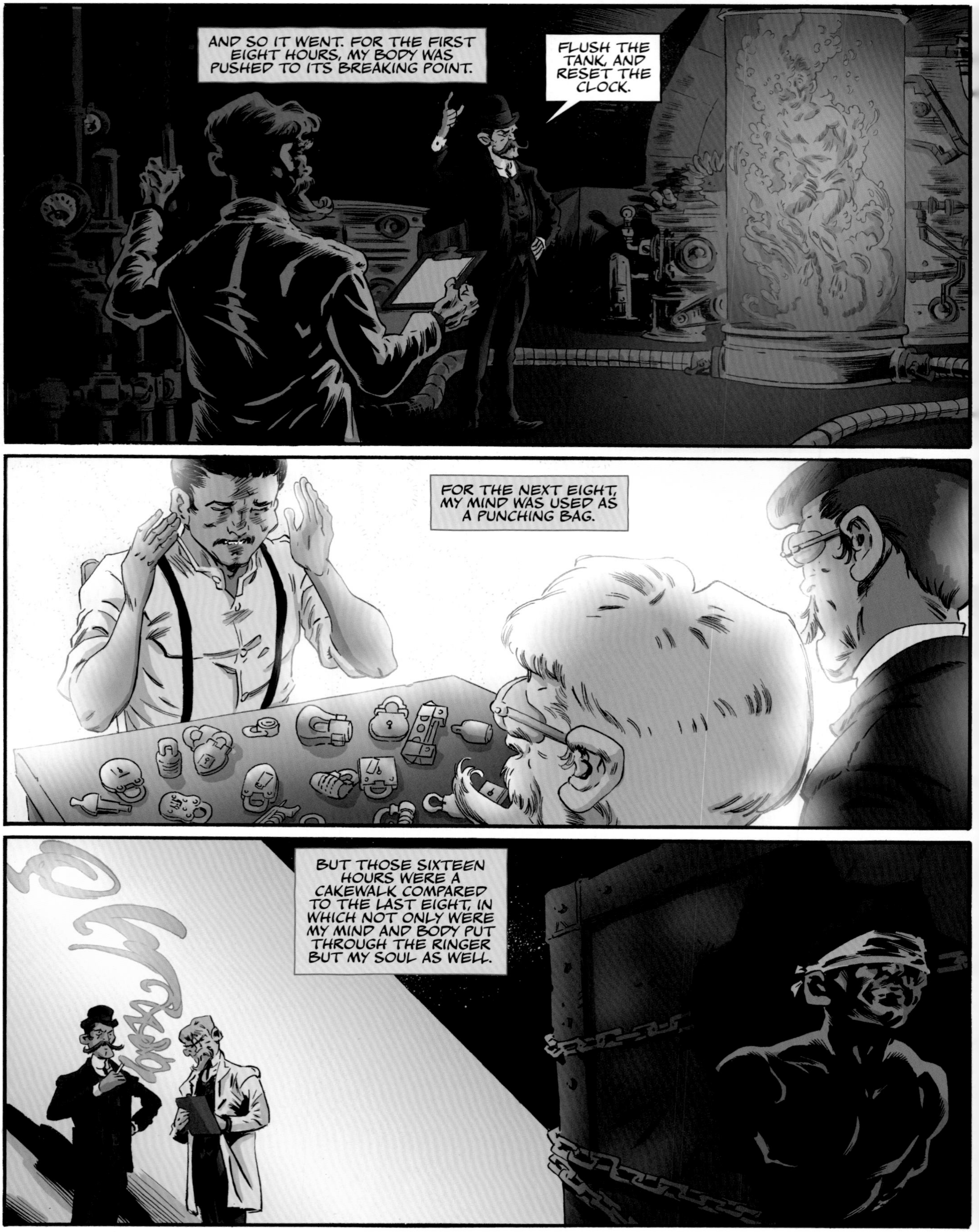
AND SO IT WENT. FOR THE FIRST EIGHT HOURS, MY BODY WAS PUSHED TO ITS BREAKING POINT.
FLUSH THE TANK, AND RESET THE CLOCK.
FOR THE NEXT EIGHT, MY MIND WAS USED AS A PUNCHING BAG.
BUT THOSE SIXTEEN HOURS WERE A CAKEWALK COMPARED TO THE LAST EIGHT, IN WHICH NOT ONLY WERE MY MIND AND BODY PUT THROUGH THE RINGER BUT MY SOUL AS WELL.

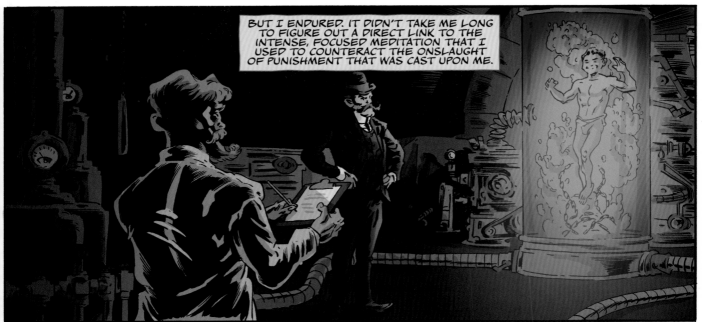

BUT I ENDURED. IT DIDN'T TAKE ME LONG TO FIGURE OUT A DIRECT LINK TO THE INTENSE, FOCUSED MEDITATION THAT I USED TO COUNTERACT THE ONSLAUGHT OF PUNISHMENT THAT WAS CAST UPON ME.

FINDING THAT BALANCE WAS THE KEY THAT GAINED ME ACCESS TO THE ENERGY'S SOURCE.

AND IN JUST ONE DAY, I UNLOCKED POWERS THAT EXCEEDED MY WILDEST DREAMS.

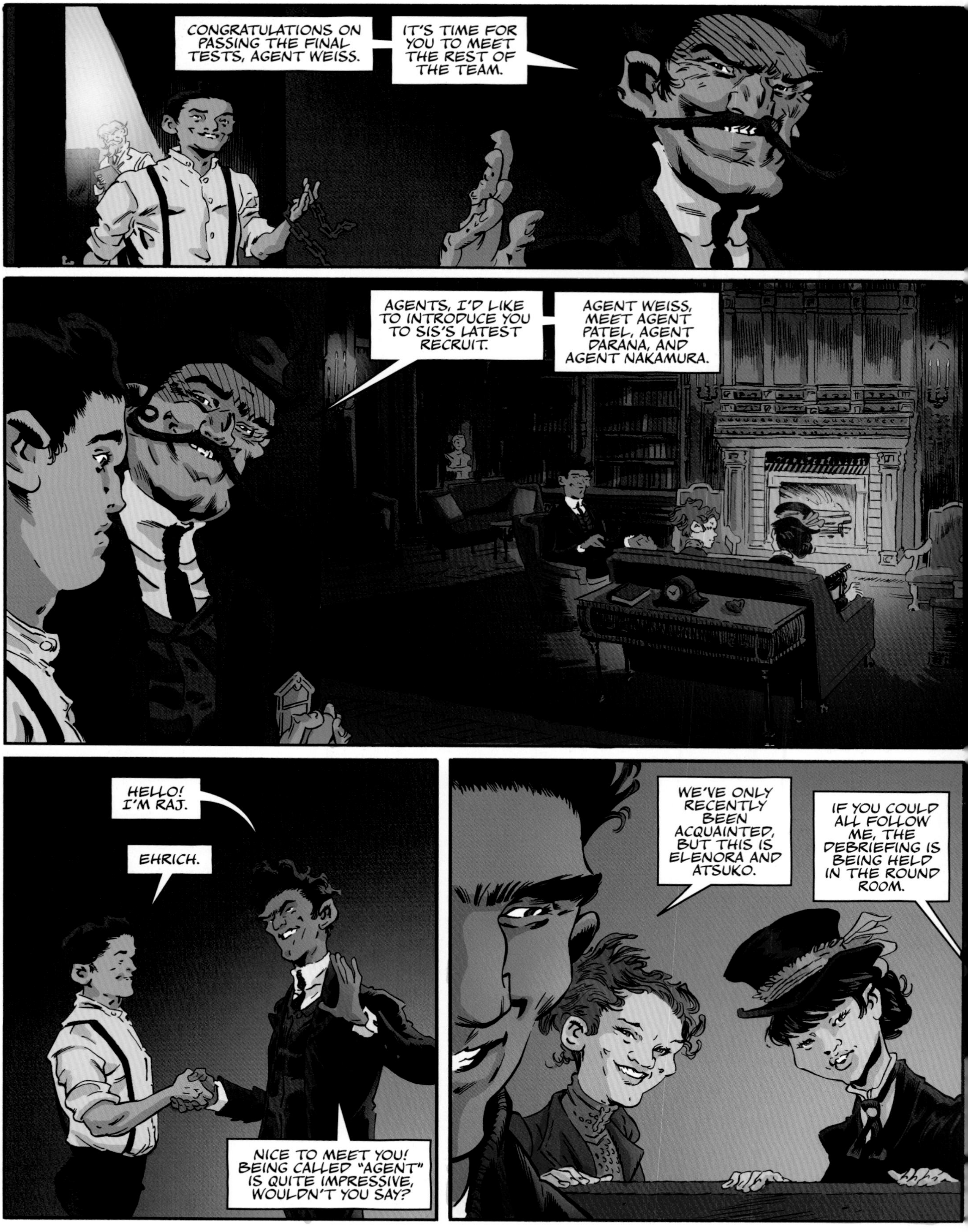
CONGRATULATIONS ON PASSING THE FINAL TESTS, AGENT WEISS.
IT'S TIME FOR YOU TO MEET THE REST OF THE TEAM.
AGENTS, I'D LIKE TO INTRODUCE YOU TO SIS'S LATEST RECRUIT.
AGENT WEISS, MEET AGENT PATEL, AGENT DARANA, AND AGENT NAKAMURA.
HELLO! I'M RAJ.
EHRICH.
NICE TO MEET YOU! BEING CALLED "AGENT" IS QUITE IMPRESSIVE, WOULDN'T YOU SAY?
WE'VE ONLY RECENTLY BEEN ACQUAINTED, BUT THIS IS ELENORA AND ATSUKO.
IF YOU COULD ALL FOLLOW ME, THE DEBRIEFING IS BEING HELD IN THE ROUND ROOM.

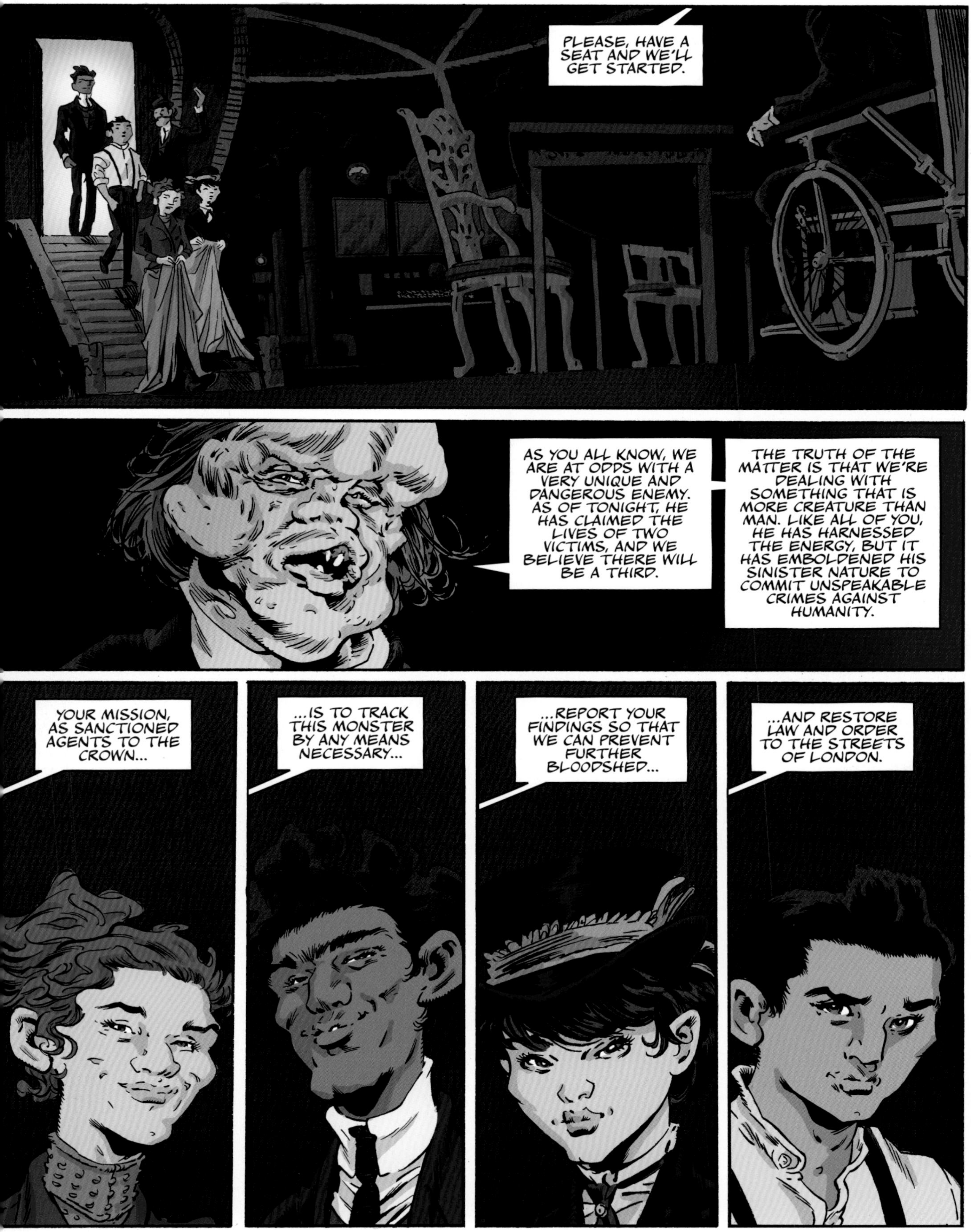

PLEASE, HAVE A SEAT AND WE'LL GET STARTED.
AS YOU ALL KNOW, WE ARE AT ODDS WITH A VERY UNIQUE AND DANGEROUS ENEMY. AS OF TONIGHT, HE HAS CLAIMED THE LIVES OF TWO VICTIMS, AND WE BELIEVE THERE WILL BE A THIRD.
THE TRUTH OF THE MATTER IS THAT WE'RE DEALING WITH SOMETHING THAT IS MORE CREATURE THAN MAN. LIKE ALL OF YOU, HE HAS HARNESSED THE ENERGY, BUT IT HAS EMBOLDENED HIS SINISTER NATURE TO COMMIT UNSPEAKABLE CRIMES AGAINST HUMANITY.
YOUR MISSION, AS SANCTIONED AGENTS TO THE CROWN...
...IS TO TRACK THIS MONSTER BY ANY MEANS NECESSARY...
...REPORT YOUR FINDINGS SO THAT WE CAN PREVENT FURTHER BLOODSHED...
...AND RESTORE LAW AND ORDER TO THE STREETS OF LONDON.

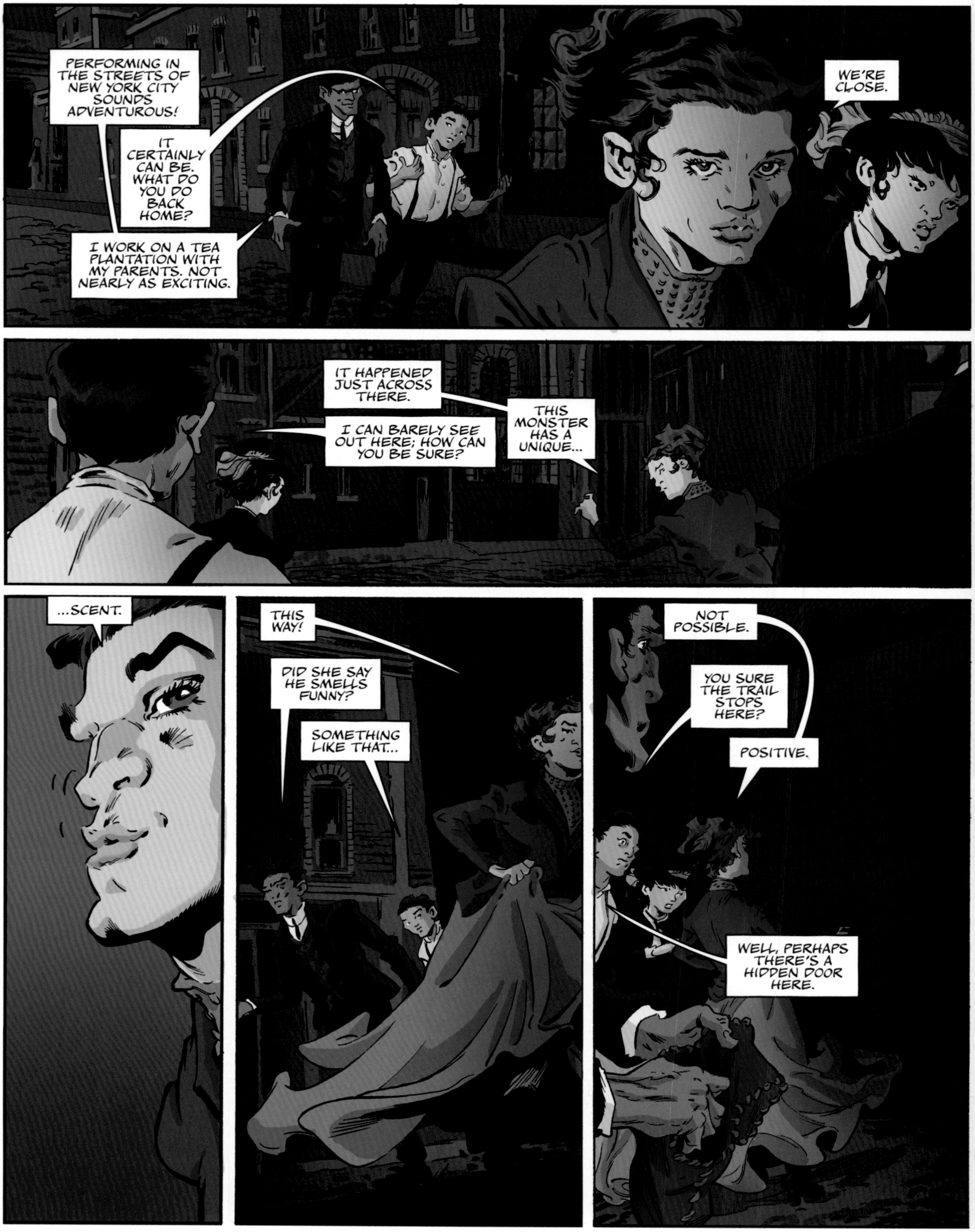
PERFORMING IN THE STREETS OF NEW YORK CITY SOUNDS ADVENTUROUS!
IT CERTAINLY CAN BE. WHAT DO YOU DO BACK HOME?
I WORK ON A TEA PLANTATION WITH MY PARENTS. NOT NEARLY AS EXCITING.
WE'RE CLOSE.
IT HAPPENED JUST ACROSS THERE.
I CAN BARELY SEE OUT HERE; HOW CAN YOU BE SURE?
THIS MONSTER HAS A UNIQUE...
...SCENT.
THIS WAY!
DID SHE SAY HE SMELLS FUNNY?
SOMETHING LIKE THAT...
NOT POSSIBLE.
YOU SURE THE TRAIL STOPS HERE?
POSITIVE.
WELL, PERHAPS THERE'S A HIDDEN DOOR HERE.

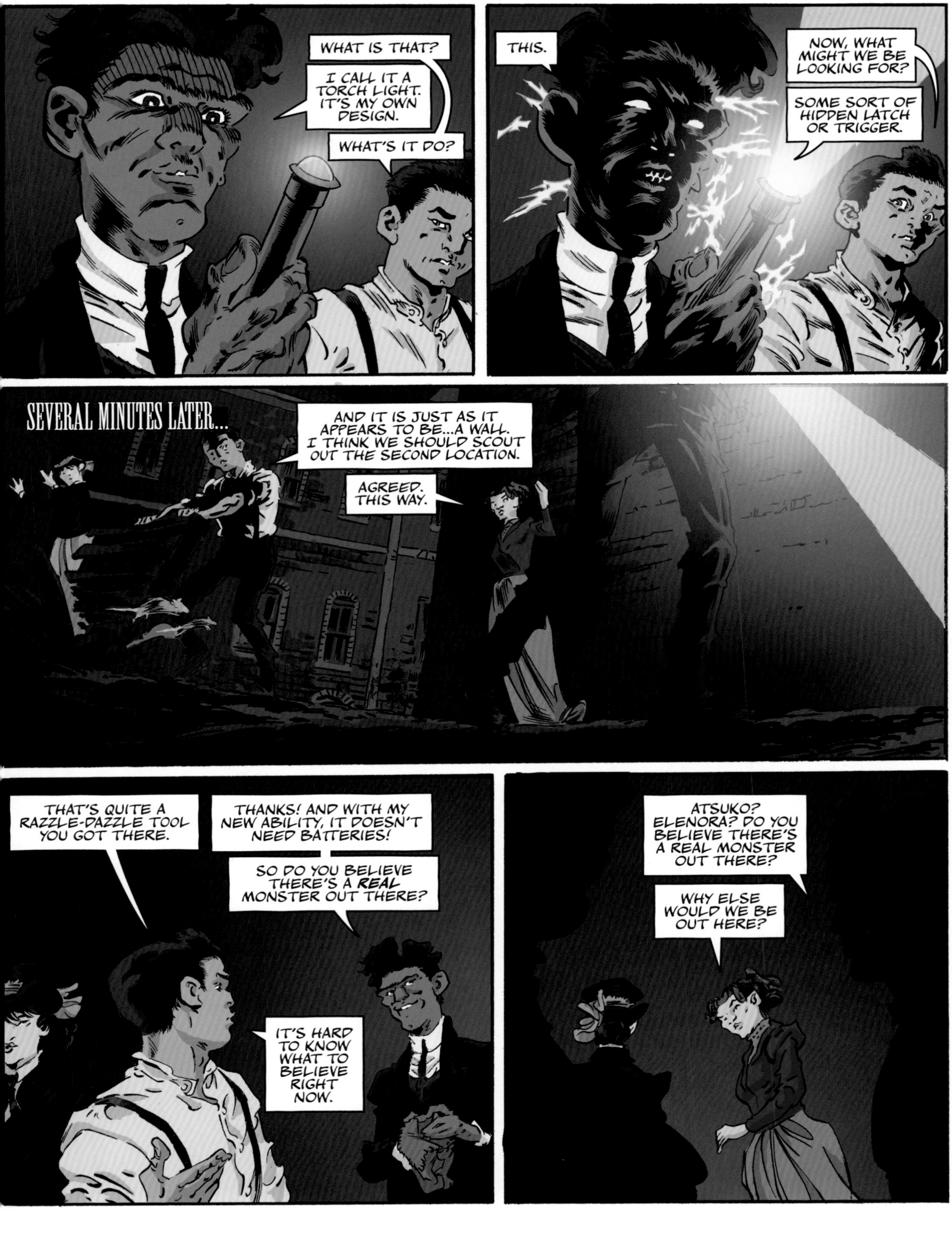
WHAT IS THAT?
I CALL IT A TORCH LIGHT. IT'S MY OWN DESIGN.
WHAT'S IT DO?
THIS.
NOW, WHAT MIGHT WE BE LOOKING FOR?
SOME SORT OF HIDDEN LATCH OR TRIGGER.
SEVERAL MINUTES LATER...
AND IT IS JUST AS IT APPEARS TO BE...A WALL. I THINK WE SHOULD SCOUT OUT THE SECOND LOCATION.
AGREED. THIS WAY.
THAT'S QUITE A RAZZLE-DAZZLE TOOL YOU GOT THERE.
THANKS! AND WITH MY NEW ABILITY, IT DOESN'T NEED BATTERIES!
SO DO YOU BELIEVE THERE'S A *REAL* MONSTER OUT THERE?
IT'S HARD TO KNOW WHAT TO BELIEVE RIGHT NOW.
ATSUKO? ELENORA? DO YOU BELIEVE THERE'S A REAL MONSTER OUT THERE?
WHY ELSE WOULD WE BE OUT HERE?

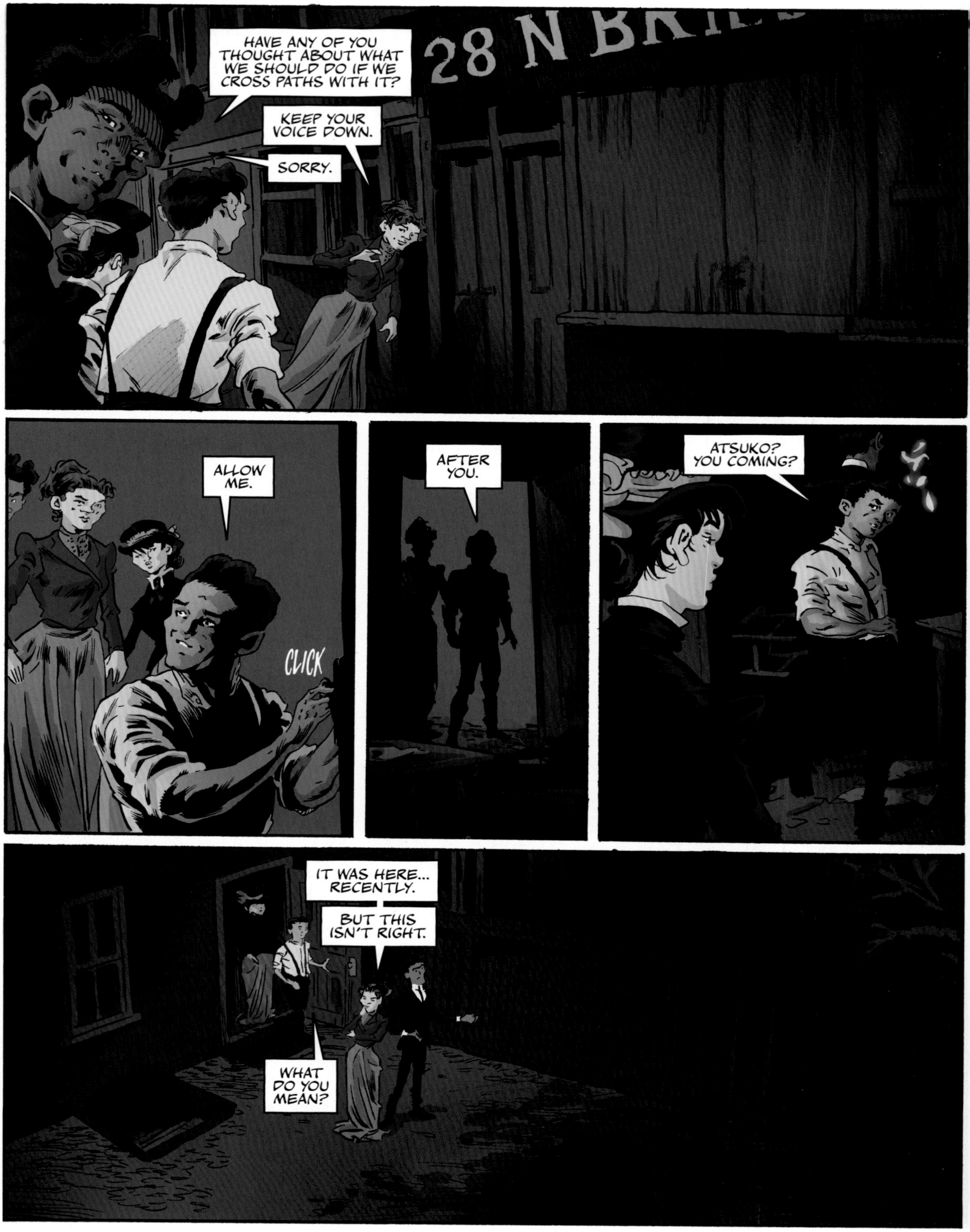

HAVE ANY OF YOU THOUGHT ABOUT WHAT WE SHOULD DO IF WE CROSS PATHS WITH IT?
KEEP YOUR VOICE DOWN.
SORRY.
28 N BR
ALLOW ME.
CLICK
AFTER YOU.
ATSUKO? YOU COMING?
IT WAS HERE... RECENTLY.
BUT THIS ISN'T RIGHT.
WHAT DO YOU MEAN?

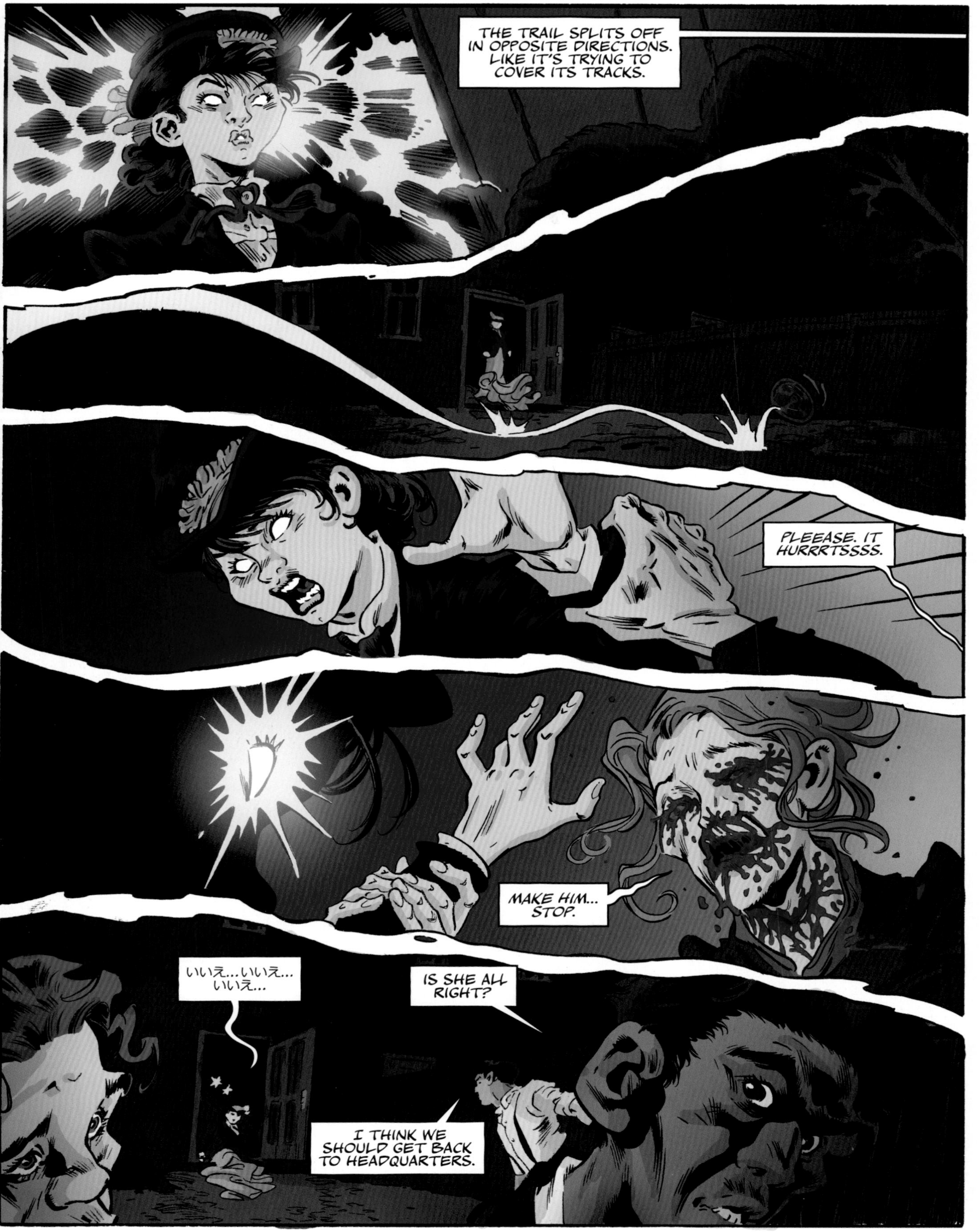
THE TRAIL SPLITS OFF IN OPPOSITE DIRECTIONS. LIKE IT'S TRYING TO COVER ITS TRACKS.
PLEEASE. IT HURRRTSSSS.
MAKE HIM... STOP.
いいえ...いいえ... いいえ...
IS SHE ALL RIGHT?
I THINK WE SHOULD GET BACK TO HEADQUARTERS.

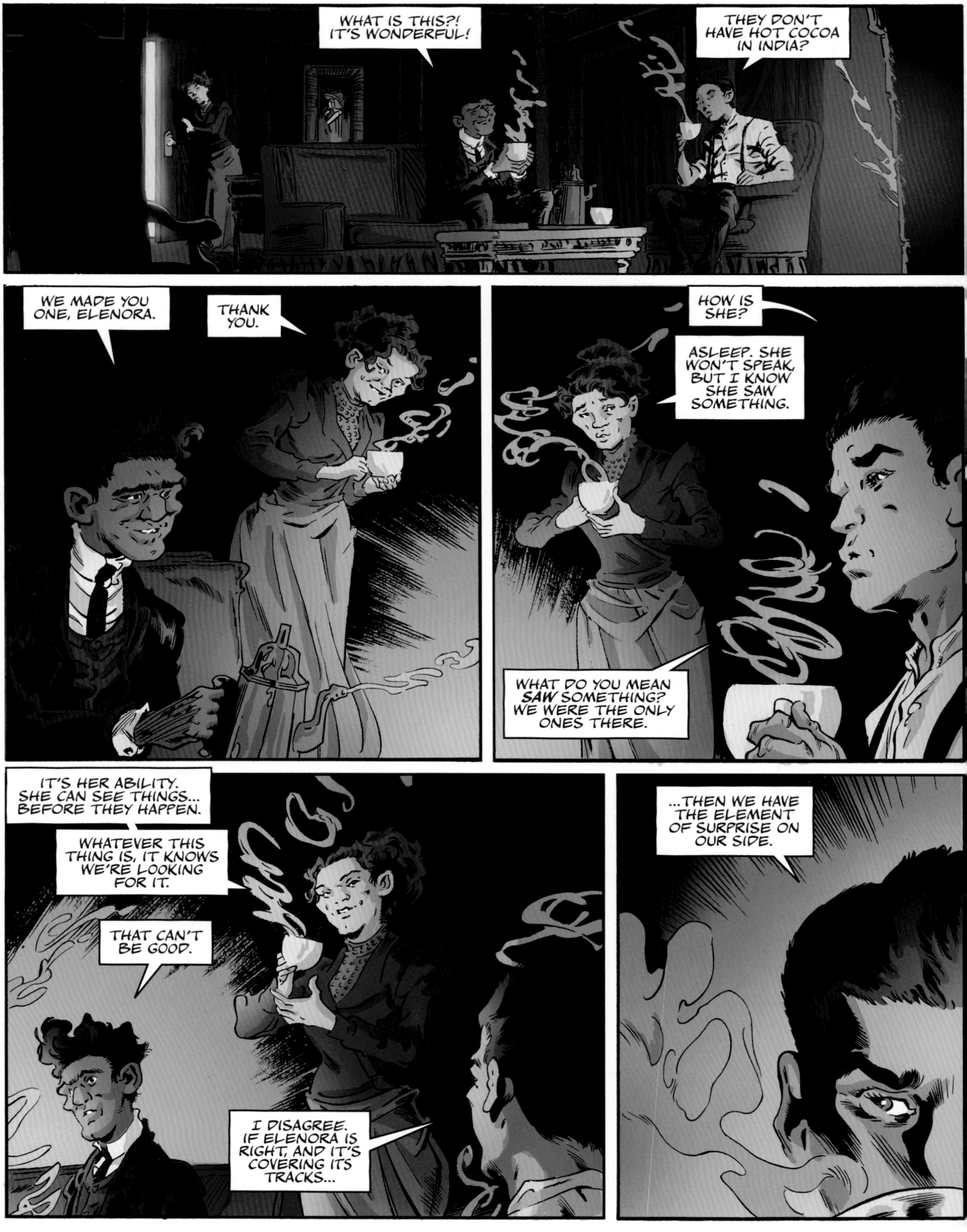
WHAT IS THIS?! IT'S WONDERFUL!
THEY DON'T HAVE HOT COCOA IN INDIA?
WE MADE YOU ONE, ELENORA.
THANK YOU.
HOW IS SHE?
ASLEEP. SHE WON'T SPEAK, BUT I KNOW SHE SAW SOMETHING.
WHAT DO YOU MEAN SAW SOMETHING? WE WERE THE ONLY ONES THERE.
IT'S HER ABILITY. SHE CAN SEE THINGS... BEFORE THEY HAPPEN.
WHATEVER THIS THING IS, IT KNOWS WE'RE LOOKING FOR IT.
THAT CAN'T BE GOOD.
I DISAGREE. IF ELENORA IS RIGHT, AND IT'S COVERING ITS TRACKS...
...THEN WE HAVE THE ELEMENT OF SURPRISE ON OUR SIDE.

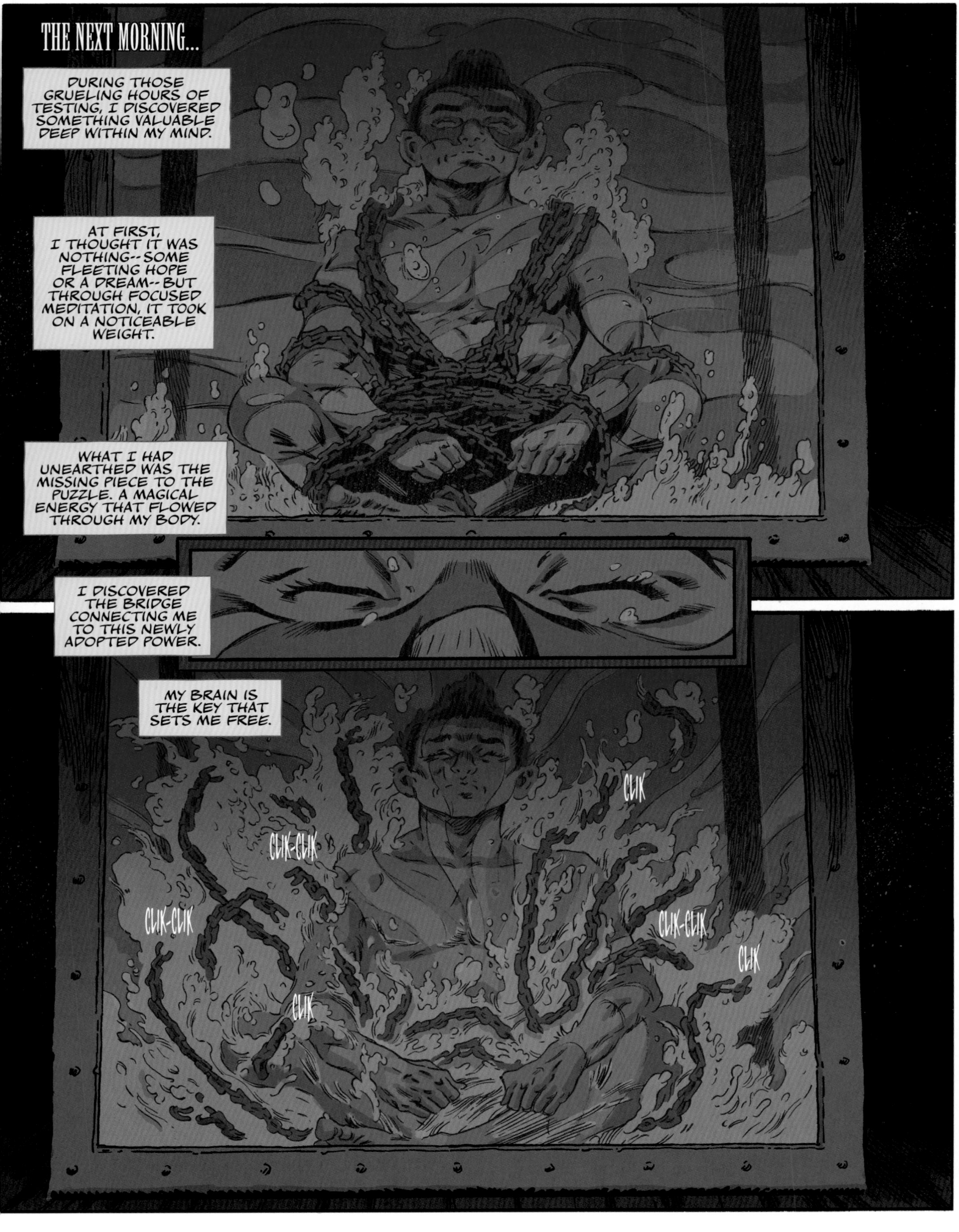
THE NEXT MORNING...
DURING THOSE GRUELING HOURS OF TESTING, I DISCOVERED SOMETHING VALUABLE DEEP WITHIN MY MIND.
AT FIRST, I THOUGHT IT WAS NOTHING--SOME FLEETING HOPE OR A DREAM--BUT THROUGH FOCUSED MEDITATION, IT TOOK ON A NOTICEABLE WEIGHT.
WHAT I HAD UNEARTHED WAS THE MISSING PIECE TO THE PUZZLE. A MAGICAL ENERGY THAT FLOWED THROUGH MY BODY.
I DISCOVERED THE BRIDGE CONNECTING ME TO THIS NEWLY ADOPTED POWER.
MY BRAIN IS THE KEY THAT SETS ME FREE.
CLIK
CLIK-CLIK
CLIK-CLIK
CLIK-CLIK
CLIK
CLIK

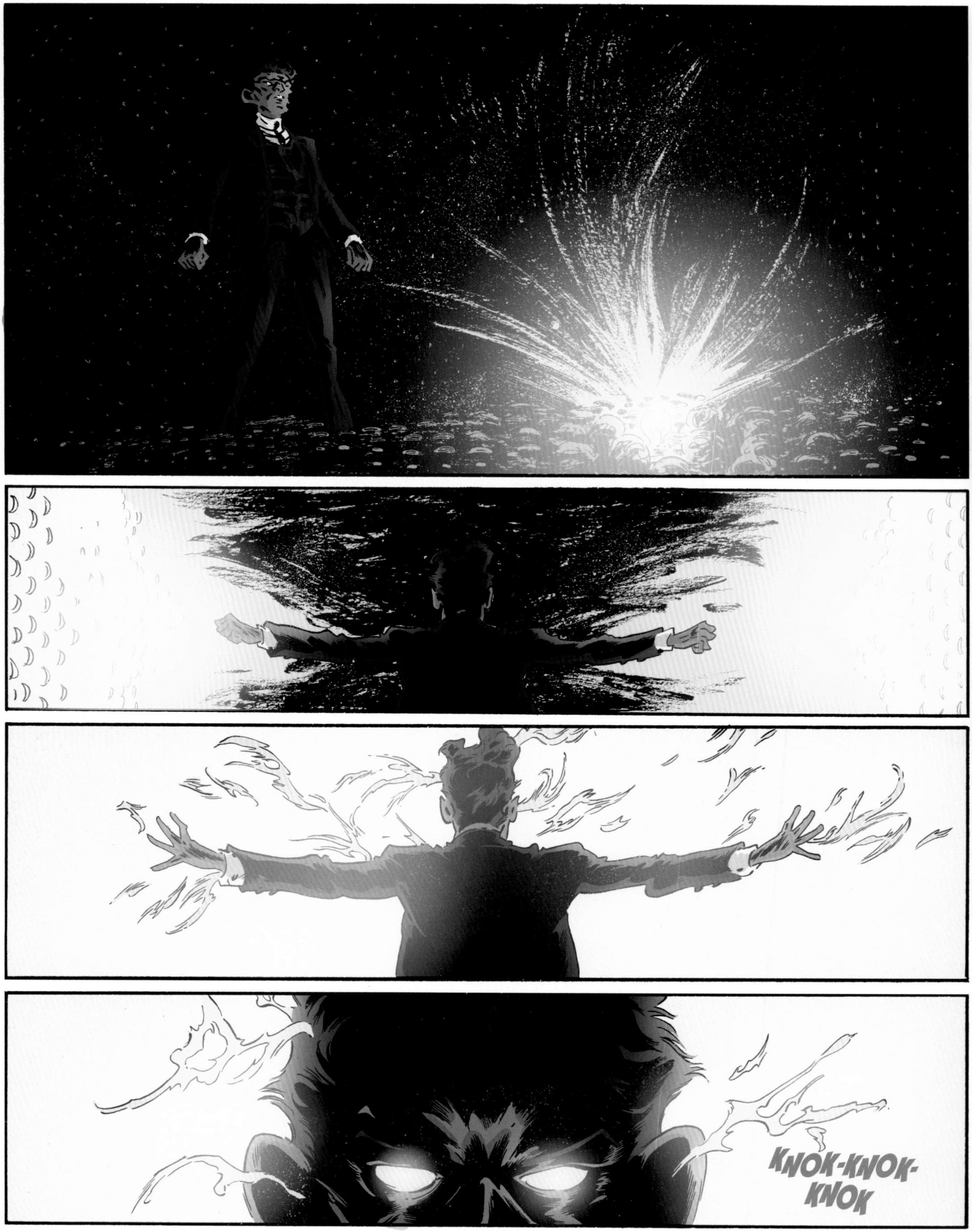
KNOK-KNOK-
KNOK

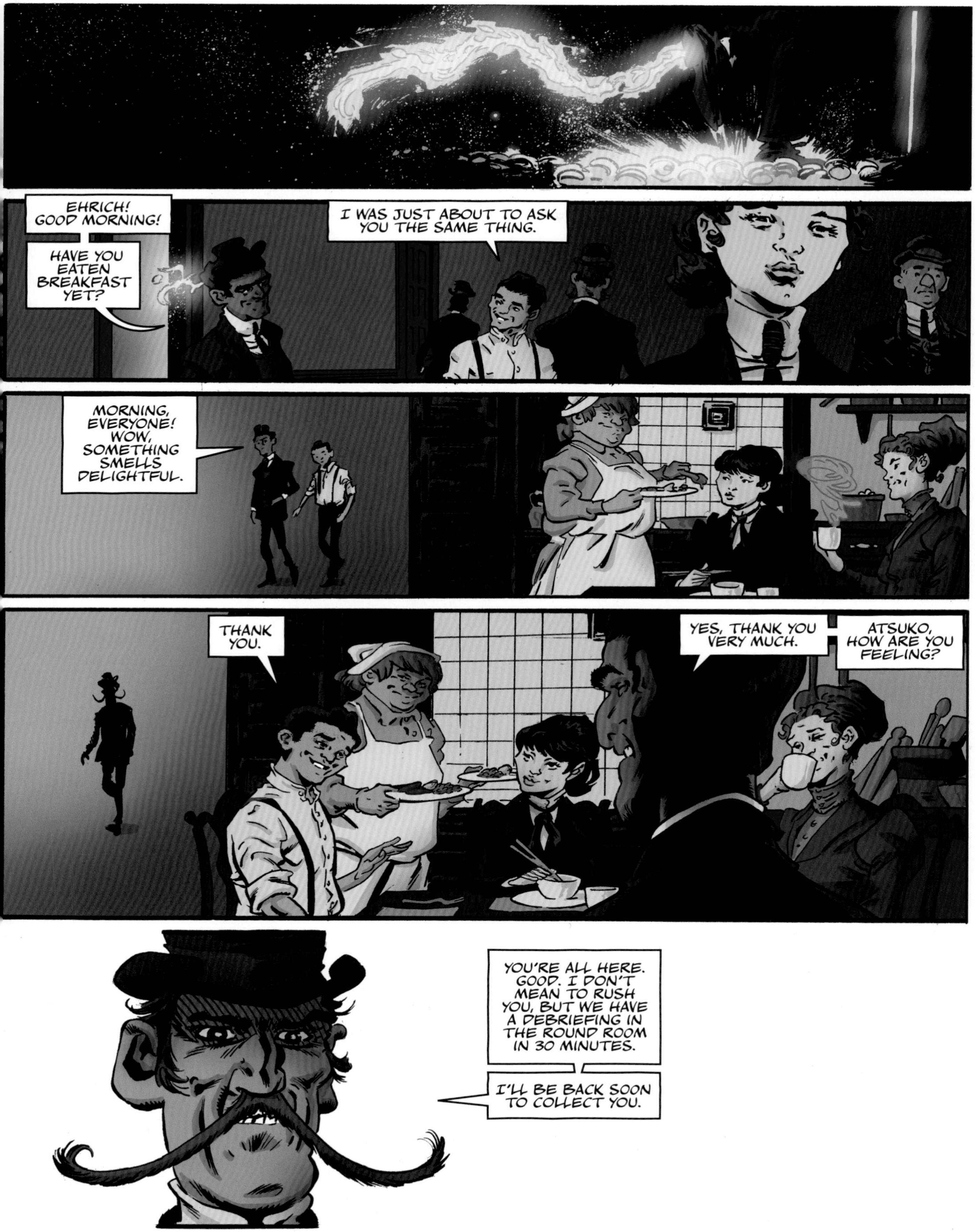
EHRICH! GOOD MORNING!
HAVE YOU EATEN BREAKFAST YET?
I WAS JUST ABOUT TO ASK YOU THE SAME THING.
MORNING, EVERYONE! WOW, SOMETHING SMELLS DELIGHTFUL.
THANK YOU.
YES, THANK YOU VERY MUCH.
ATSUKO, HOW ARE YOU FEELING?
YOU'RE ALL HERE. GOOD. I DON'T MEAN TO RUSH YOU, BUT WE HAVE A DEBRIEFING IN THE ROUND ROOM IN 30 MINUTES.
I'LL BE BACK SOON TO COLLECT YOU.

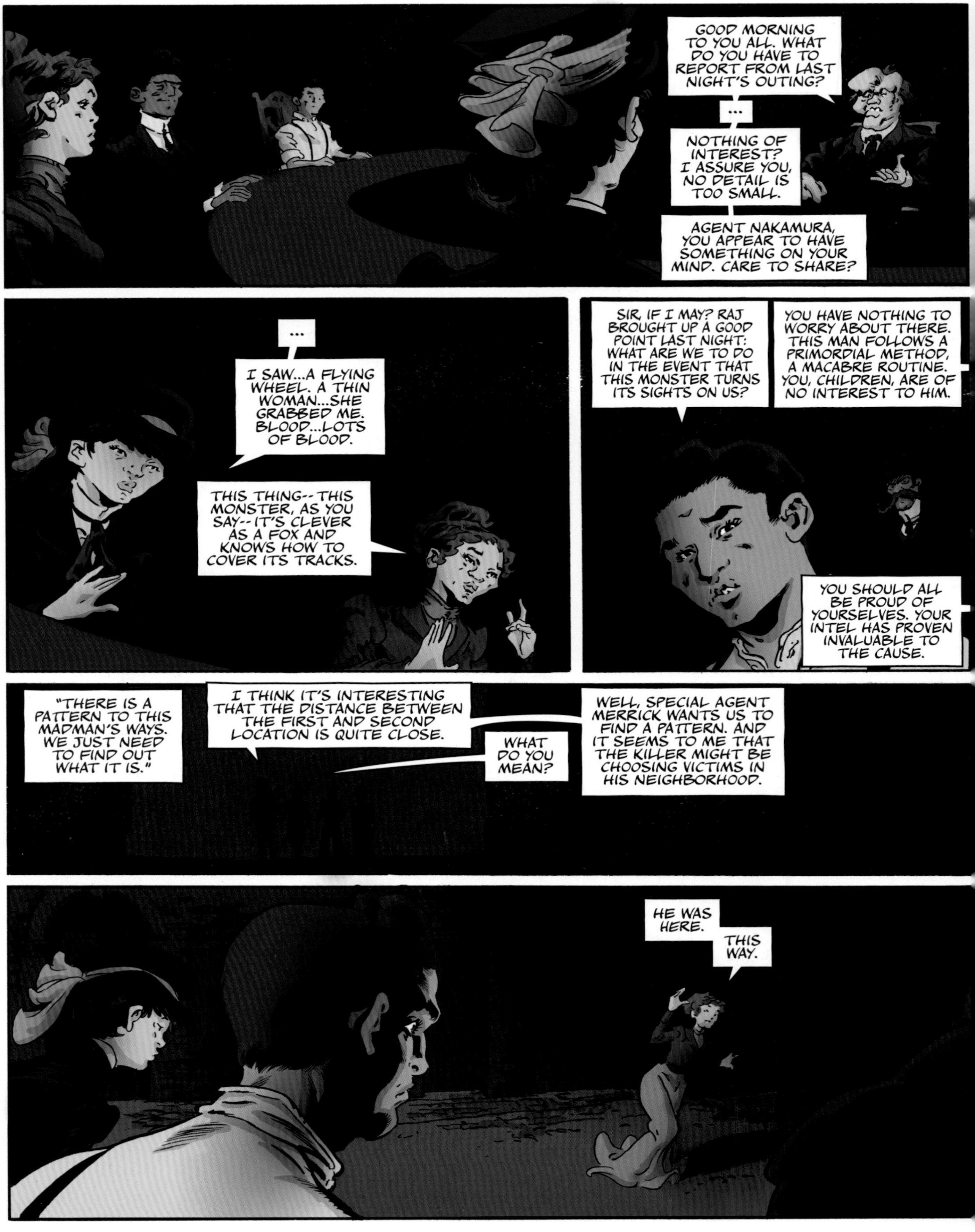
GOOD MORNING TO YOU ALL. WHAT DO YOU HAVE TO REPORT FROM LAST NIGHT'S OUTING?
...
NOTHING OF INTEREST? I ASSURE YOU, NO DETAIL IS TOO SMALL.
AGENT NAKAMURA, YOU APPEAR TO HAVE SOMETHING ON YOUR MIND. CARE TO SHARE?
...
I SAW...A FLYING WHEEL. A THIN WOMAN...SHE GRABBED ME. BLOOD...LOTS OF BLOOD.
THIS THING--THIS MONSTER, AS YOU SAY--IT'S CLEVER AS A FOX AND KNOWS HOW TO COVER ITS TRACKS.
SIR, IF I MAY? RAJ BROUGHT UP A GOOD POINT LAST NIGHT: WHAT ARE WE TO DO IN THE EVENT THAT THIS MONSTER TURNS ITS SIGHTS ON US?
YOU HAVE NOTHING TO WORRY ABOUT THERE. THIS MAN FOLLOWS A PRIMORDIAL METHOD, A MACABRE ROUTINE. YOU, CHILDREN, ARE OF NO INTEREST TO HIM.
YOU SHOULD ALL BE PROUD OF YOURSELVES. YOUR INTEL HAS PROVEN INVALUABLE TO THE CAUSE.
"THERE IS A PATTERN TO THIS MADMAN'S WAYS. WE JUST NEED TO FIND OUT WHAT IT IS."
I THINK IT'S INTERESTING THAT THE DISTANCE BETWEEN THE FIRST AND SECOND LOCATION IS QUITE CLOSE.
WHAT DO YOU MEAN?
WELL, SPECIAL AGENT MERRICK WANTS US TO FIND A PATTERN. AND IT SEEMS TO ME THAT THE KILLER MIGHT BE CHOOSING VICTIMS IN HIS NEIGHBORHOOD.
HE WAS HERE.
THIS WAY.

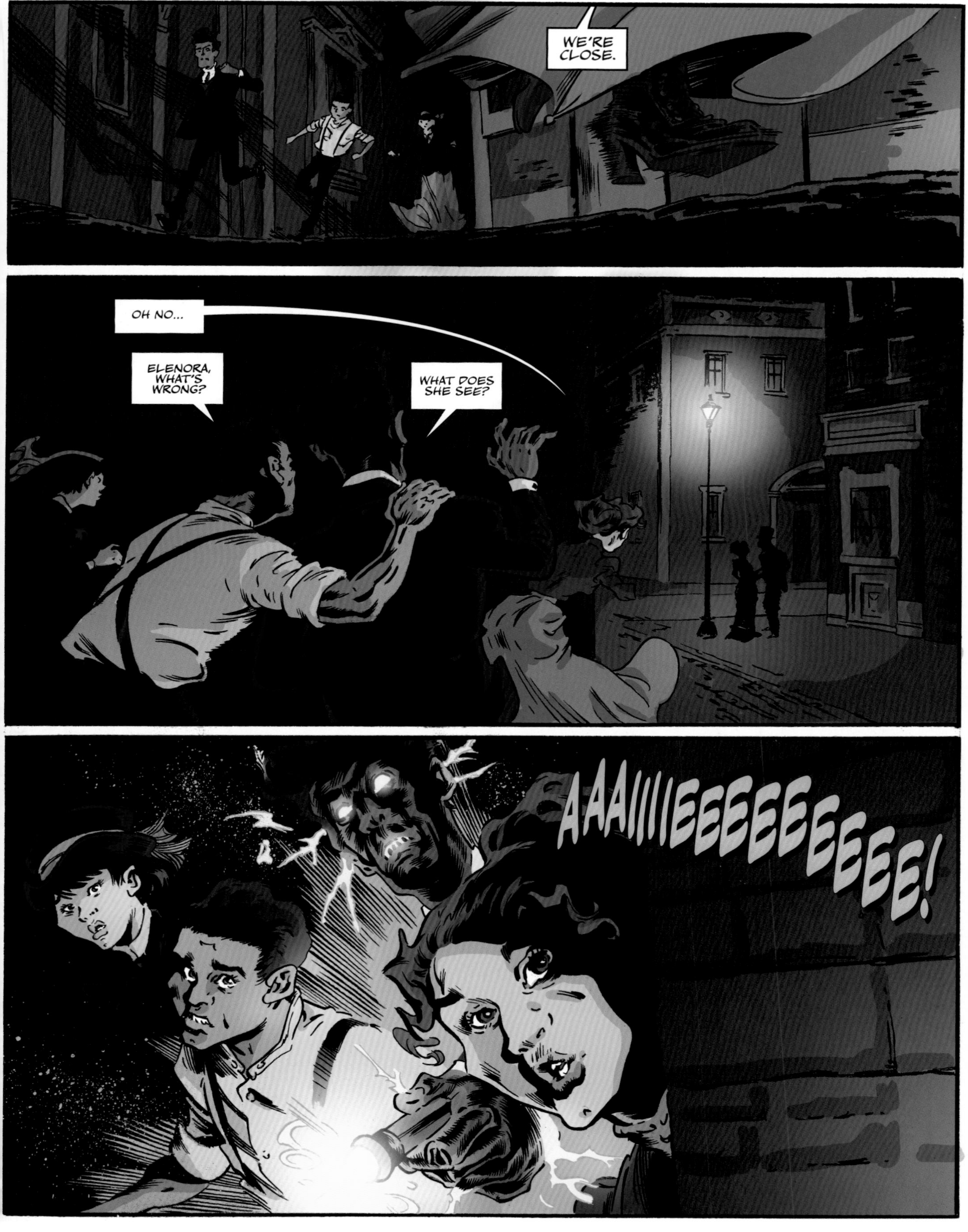
WE'RE CLOSE.
OH NO...
ELENORA, WHAT'S WRONG?
WHAT DOES SHE SEE?
AAAIIIIIEEEEEEEEEEE!

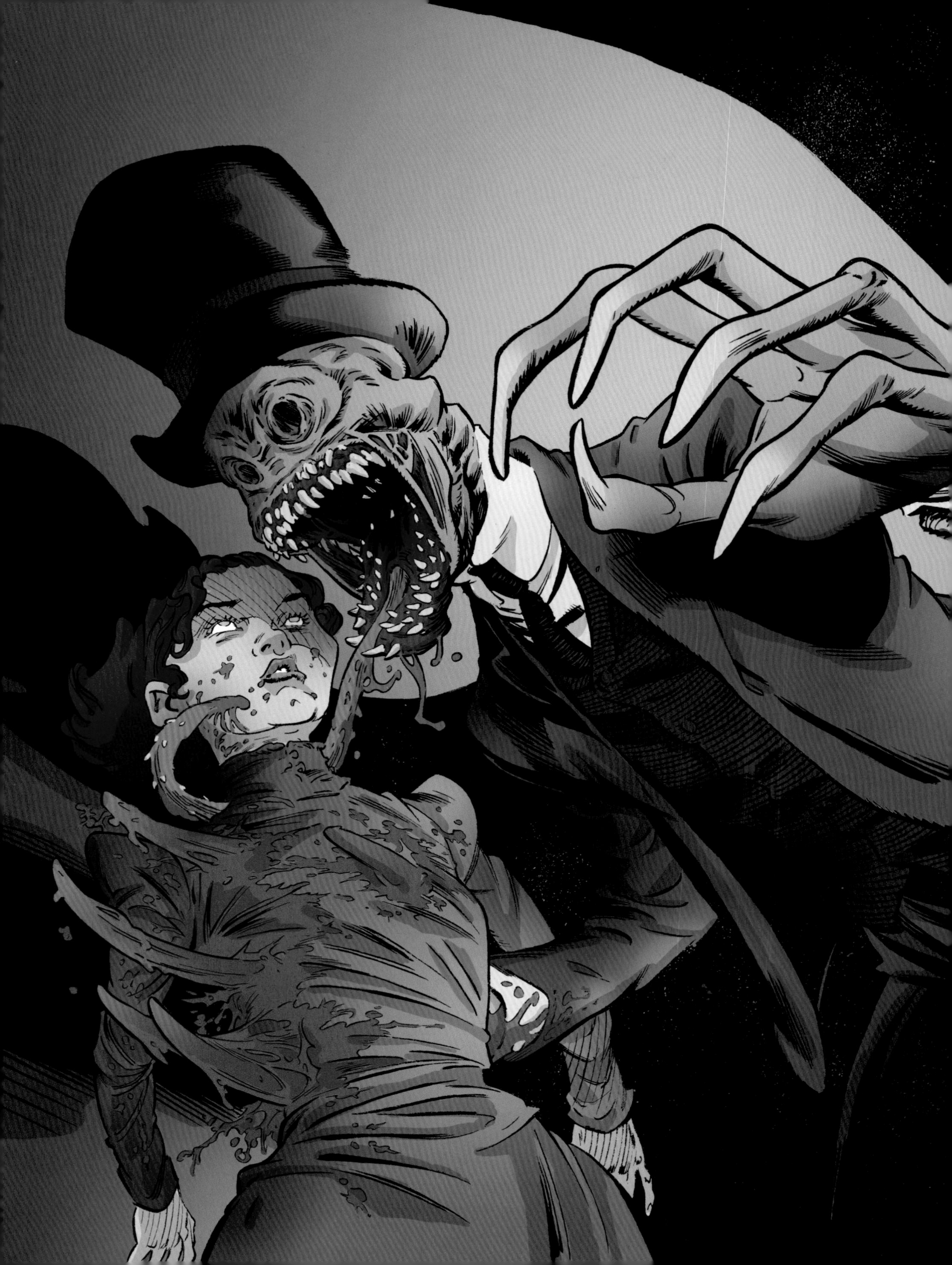

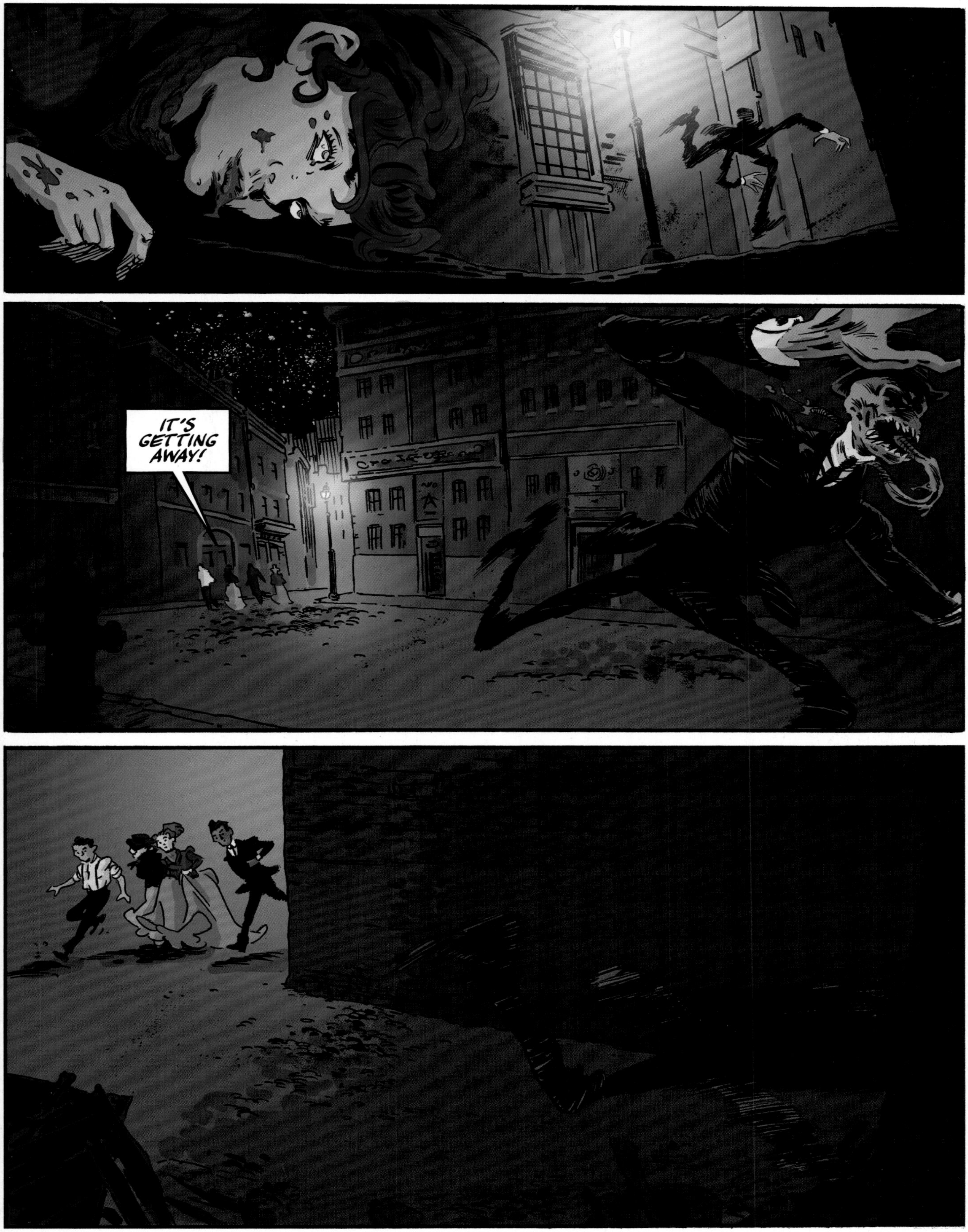
IT'S GETTING AWAY!

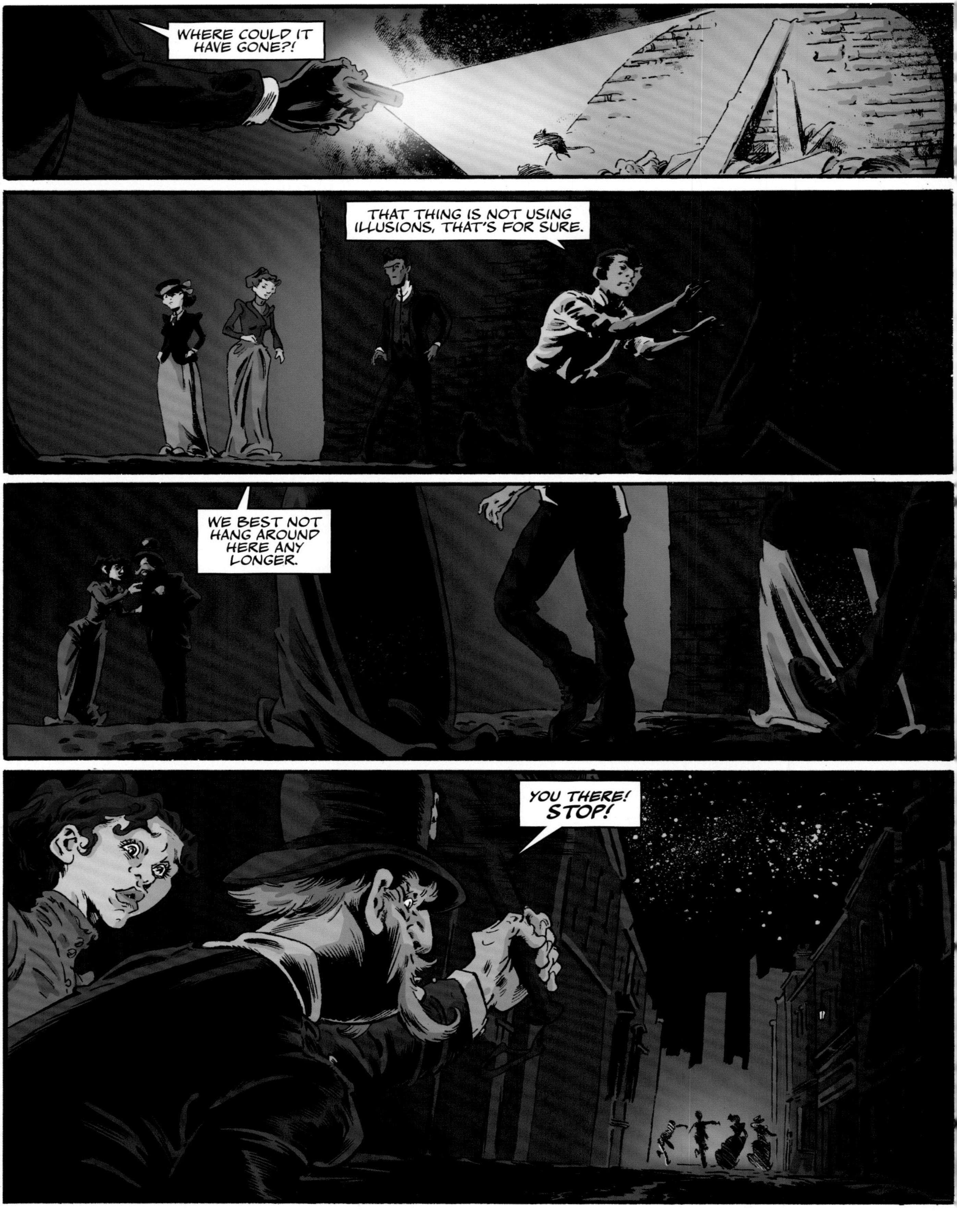
WHERE COULD IT HAVE GONE?!
THAT THING IS NOT USING ILLUSIONS, THAT'S FOR SURE.
WE BEST NOT HANG AROUND HERE ANY LONGER.
YOU THERE! STOP!

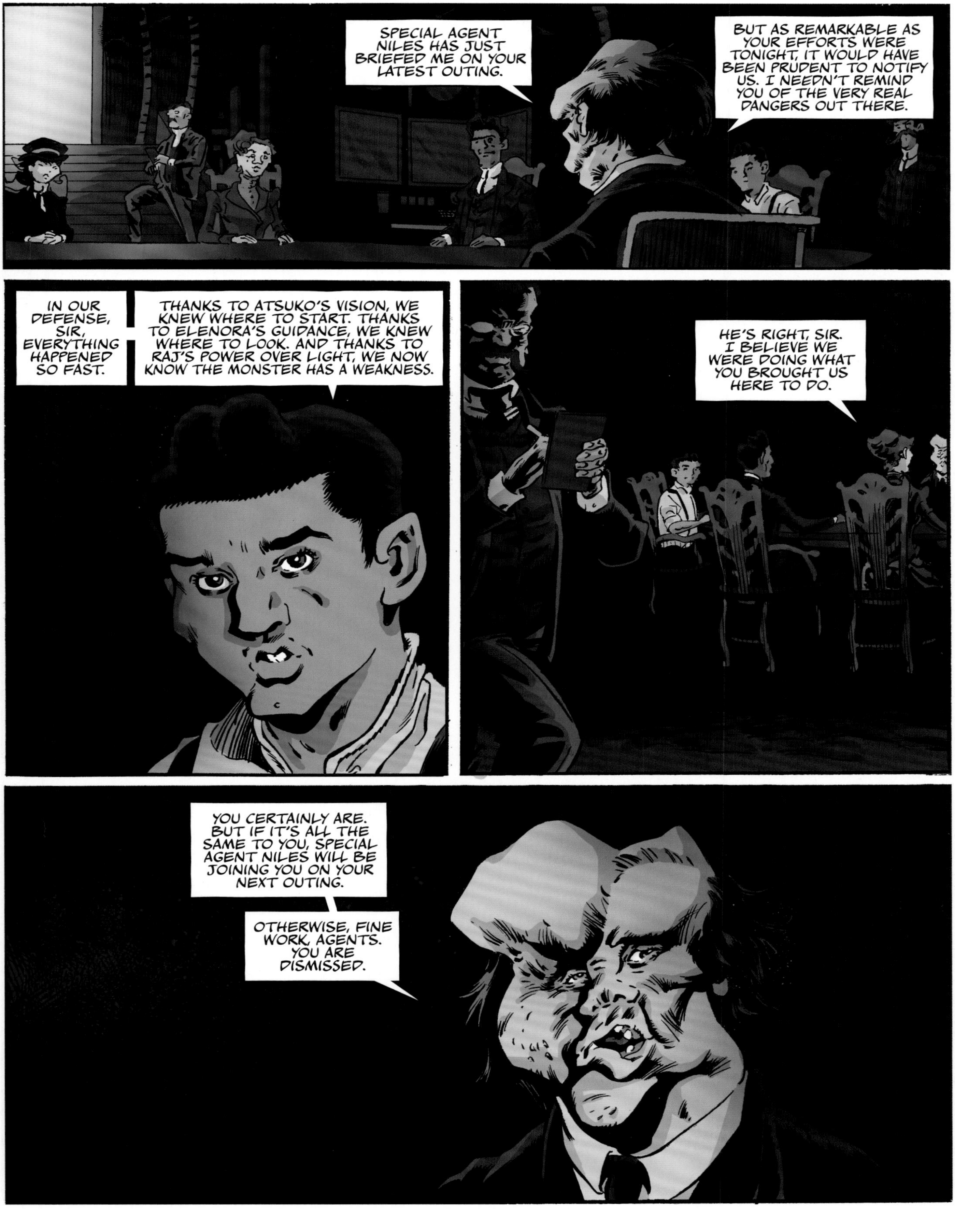
SPECIAL AGENT NILES HAS JUST BRIEFED ME ON YOUR LATEST OUTING.
BUT AS REMARKABLE AS YOUR EFFORTS WERE TONIGHT, IT WOULD HAVE BEEN PRUDENT TO NOTIFY US. I NEEDN'T REMIND YOU OF THE VERY REAL DANGERS OUT THERE.
IN OUR DEFENSE, SIR, EVERYTHING HAPPENED SO FAST.
THANKS TO ATSUKO'S VISION, WE KNEW WHERE TO START. THANKS TO ELENORA'S GUIDANCE, WE KNEW WHERE TO LOOK. AND THANKS TO RAJ'S POWER OVER LIGHT, WE NOW KNOW THE MONSTER HAS A WEAKNESS.
HE'S RIGHT, SIR. I BELIEVE WE WERE DOING WHAT YOU BROUGHT US HERE TO DO.
YOU CERTAINLY ARE. BUT IF IT'S ALL THE SAME TO YOU, SPECIAL AGENT NILES WILL BE JOINING YOU ON YOUR NEXT OUTING.
OTHERWISE, FINE WORK, AGENTS. YOU ARE DISMISSED.

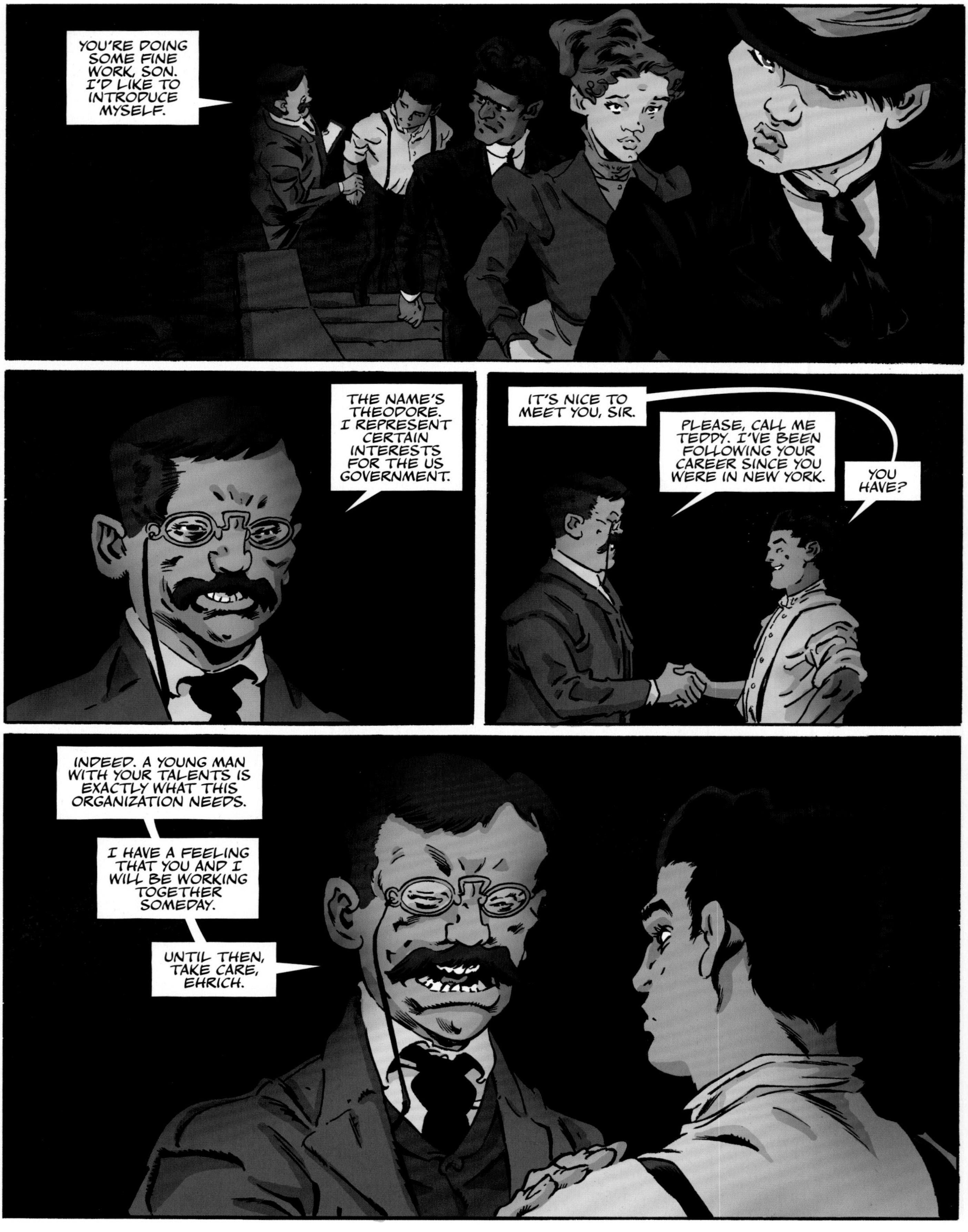

YOU'RE DOING SOME FINE WORK, SON. I'D LIKE TO INTRODUCE MYSELF.
THE NAME'S THEODORE. I REPRESENT CERTAIN INTERESTS FOR THE US GOVERNMENT.
IT'S NICE TO MEET YOU, SIR.
PLEASE, CALL ME TEDDY. I'VE BEEN FOLLOWING YOUR CAREER SINCE YOU WERE IN NEW YORK.
YOU HAVE?
INDEED. A YOUNG MAN WITH YOUR TALENTS IS EXACTLY WHAT THIS ORGANIZATION NEEDS.
I HAVE A FEELING THAT YOU AND I WILL BE WORKING TOGETHER SOMEDAY.
UNTIL THEN, TAKE CARE, EHRICH.

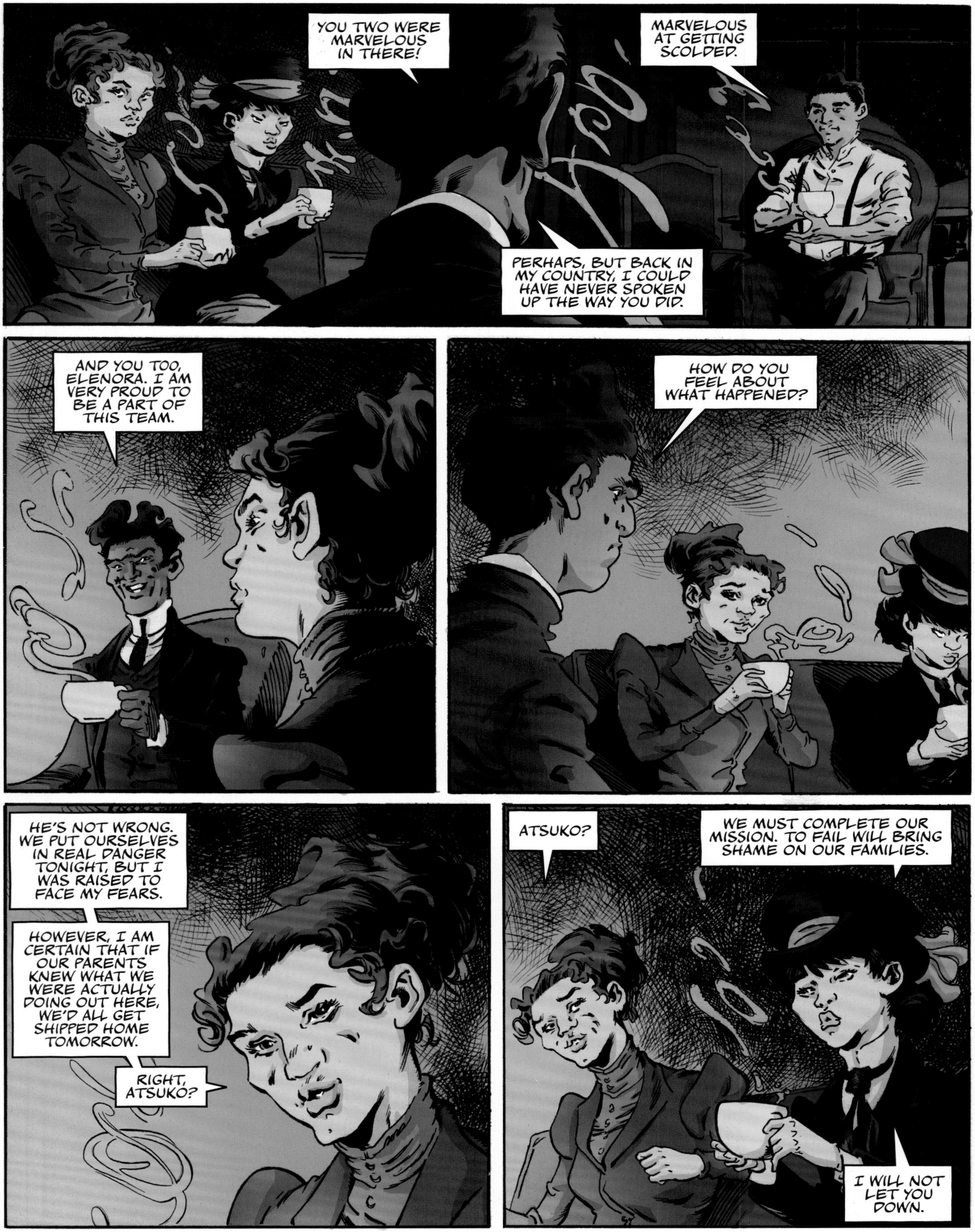
YOU TWO WERE MARVELOUS IN THERE!
MARVELOUS AT GETTING SCOLDED.
PERHAPS, BUT BACK IN MY COUNTRY, I COULD HAVE NEVER SPOKEN UP THE WAY YOU DID.
AND YOU TOO, ELENORA. I AM VERY PROUD TO BE A PART OF THIS TEAM.
HOW DO YOU FEEL ABOUT WHAT HAPPENED?
HE'S NOT WRONG. WE PUT OURSELVES IN REAL DANGER TONIGHT, BUT I WAS RAISED TO FACE MY FEARS.
HOWEVER, I AM CERTAIN THAT IF OUR PARENTS KNEW WHAT WE WERE ACTUALLY DOING OUT HERE, WE'D ALL GET SHIPPED HOME TOMORROW.
RIGHT, ATSUKO?
ATSUKO?
WE MUST COMPLETE OUR MISSION. TO FAIL WILL BRING SHAME ON OUR FAMILIES.
I WILL NOT LET YOU DOWN.

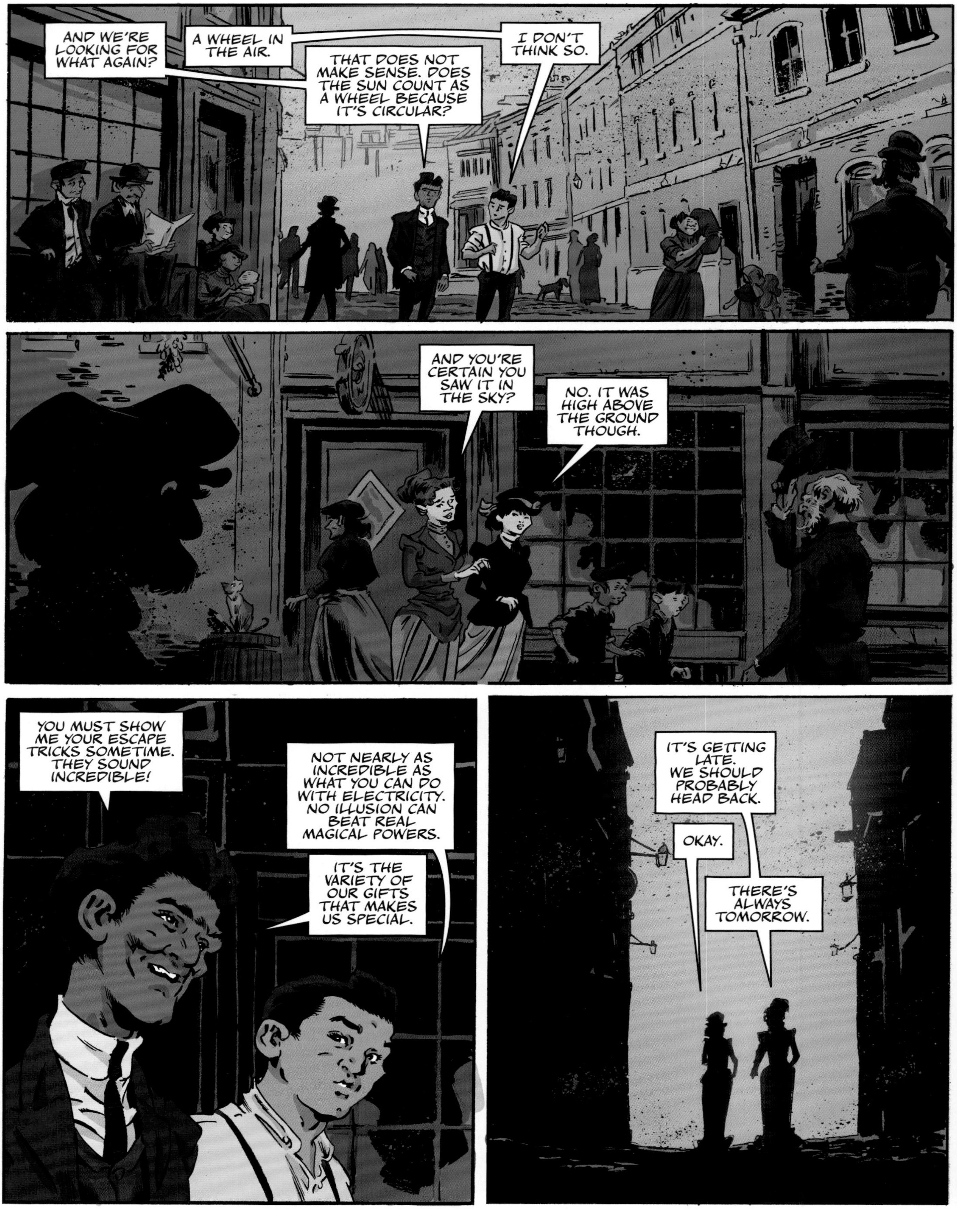
AND WE'RE LOOKING FOR WHAT AGAIN?
A WHEEL IN THE AIR.
THAT DOES NOT MAKE SENSE. DOES THE SUN COUNT AS A WHEEL BECAUSE IT'S CIRCULAR?
I DON'T THINK SO.
AND YOU'RE CERTAIN YOU SAW IT IN THE SKY?
NO. IT WAS HIGH ABOVE THE GROUND THOUGH.
YOU MUST SHOW ME YOUR ESCAPE TRICKS SOMETIME. THEY SOUND INCREDIBLE!
NOT NEARLY AS INCREDIBLE AS WHAT YOU CAN DO WITH ELECTRICITY. NO ILLUSION CAN BEAT REAL MAGICAL POWERS.
IT'S THE VARIETY OF OUR GIFTS THAT MAKES US SPECIAL.
IT'S GETTING LATE. WE SHOULD PROBABLY HEAD BACK.
OKAY.
THERE'S ALWAYS TOMORROW.

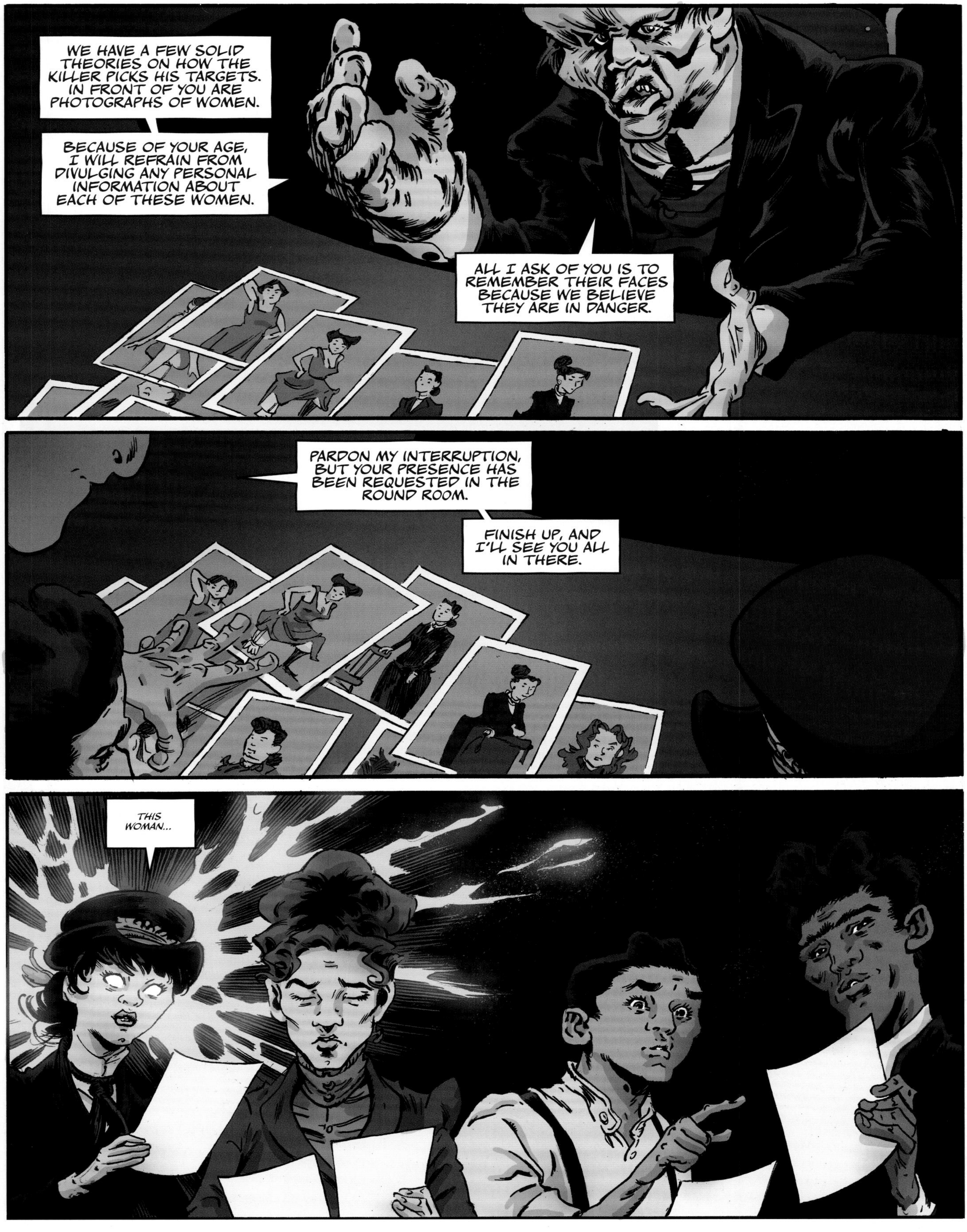
WE HAVE A FEW SOLID THEORIES ON HOW THE KILLER PICKS HIS TARGETS. IN FRONT OF YOU ARE PHOTOGRAPHS OF WOMEN.
BECAUSE OF YOUR AGE, I WILL REFRAIN FROM DIVULGING ANY PERSONAL INFORMATION ABOUT EACH OF THESE WOMEN.
ALL I ASK OF YOU IS TO REMEMBER THEIR FACES BECAUSE WE BELIEVE THEY ARE IN DANGER.
PARDON MY INTERRUPTION, BUT YOUR PRESENCE HAS BEEN REQUESTED IN THE ROUND ROOM.
FINISH UP, AND I'LL SEE YOU ALL IN THERE.
THIS WOMAN...

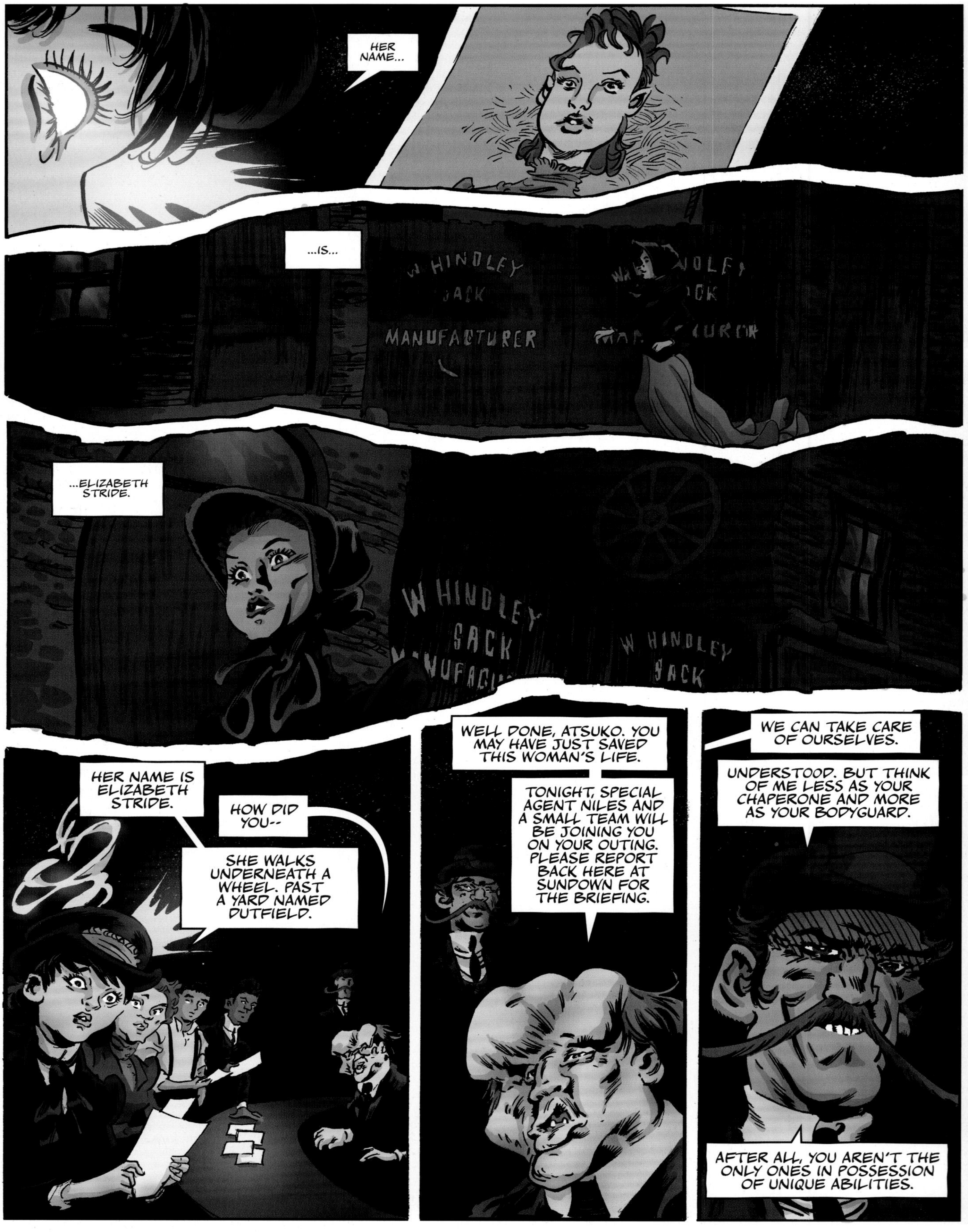

HER NAME...
...IS...
W HINDLEY SACK MANUFACTURER
...ELIZABETH STRIDE.
W HINDLEY SACK
W HINDLEY SACK
HER NAME IS ELIZABETH STRIDE.
HOW DID YOU--
SHE WALKS UNDERNEATH A WHEEL. PAST A YARD NAMED DUTFIELD.
WELL DONE, ATSUKO. YOU MAY HAVE JUST SAVED THIS WOMAN'S LIFE.
TONIGHT, SPECIAL AGENT NILES AND A SMALL TEAM WILL BE JOINING YOU ON YOUR OUTING. PLEASE REPORT BACK HERE AT SUNDOWN FOR THE BRIEFING.
WE CAN TAKE CARE OF OURSELVES.
UNDERSTOOD. BUT THINK OF ME LESS AS YOUR CHAPERONE AND MORE AS YOUR BODYGUARD.
AFTER ALL, YOU AREN'T THE ONLY ONES IN POSSESSION OF UNIQUE ABILITIES.

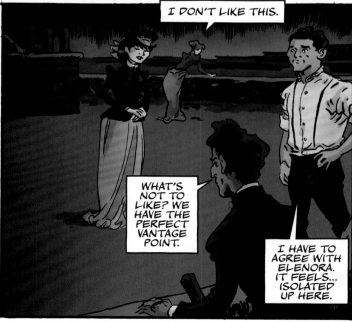

I DON'T LIKE THIS.

WHAT'S NOT TO LIKE? WE HAVE THE PERFECT VANTAGE POINT.

I HAVE TO AGREE WITH ELENORA. IT FEELS... ISOLATED UP HERE.

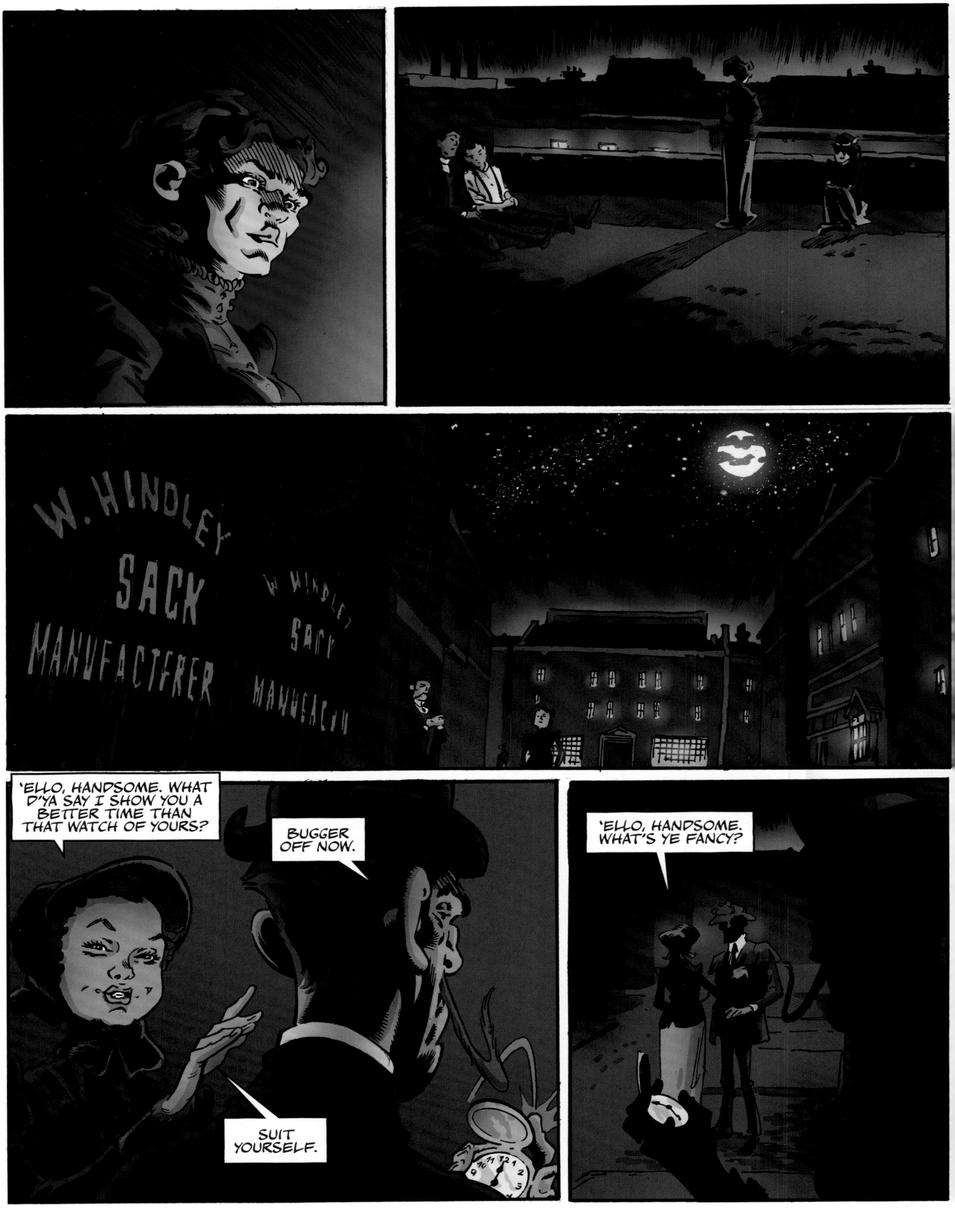
W. HINDLEY
SACK
MANUFACTERER
'ELLO, HANDSOME. WHAT D'YA SAY I SHOW YOU A BETTER TIME THAN THAT WATCH OF YOURS?
BUGGER OFF NOW.
SUIT YOURSELF.
'ELLO, HANDSOME. WHAT'S YE FANCY?

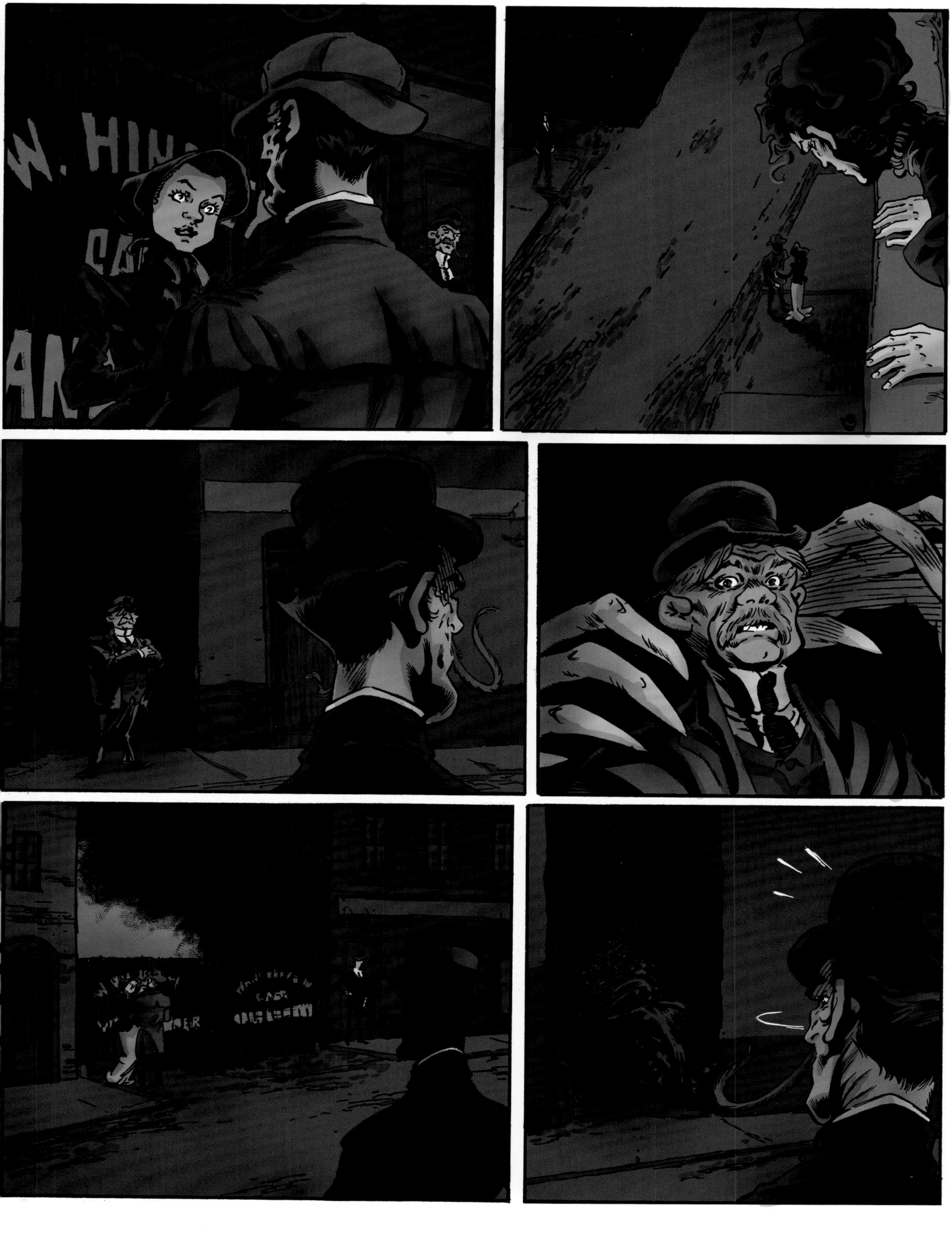

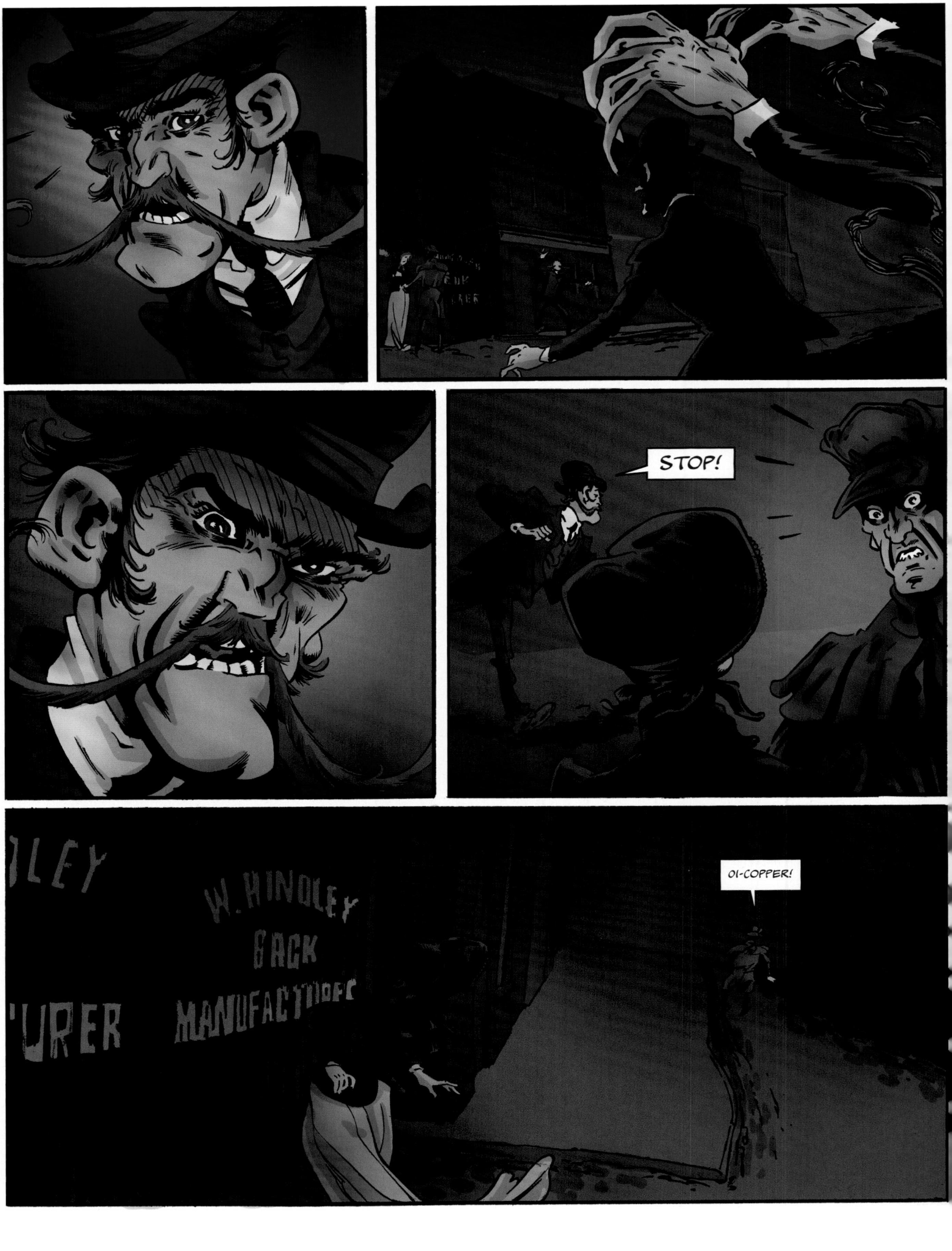
STOP!
OLEY
URER
W. HINDLEY
SACK
MANUFACTURER
OI-COPPER!

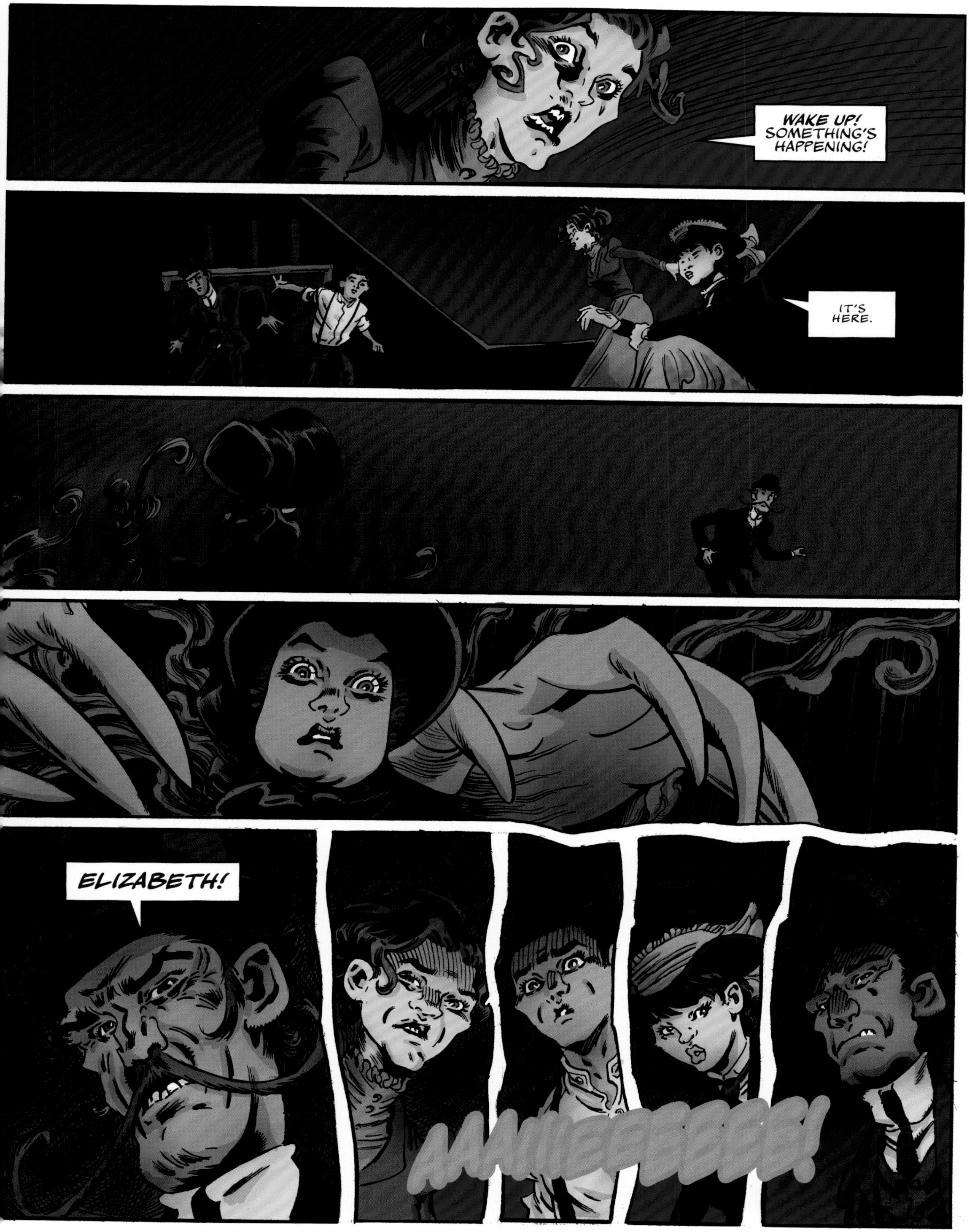

WAKE UP! SOMETHING'S HAPPENING!
IT'S HERE.
ELIZABETH!
AAAIIIEEEEEEE!

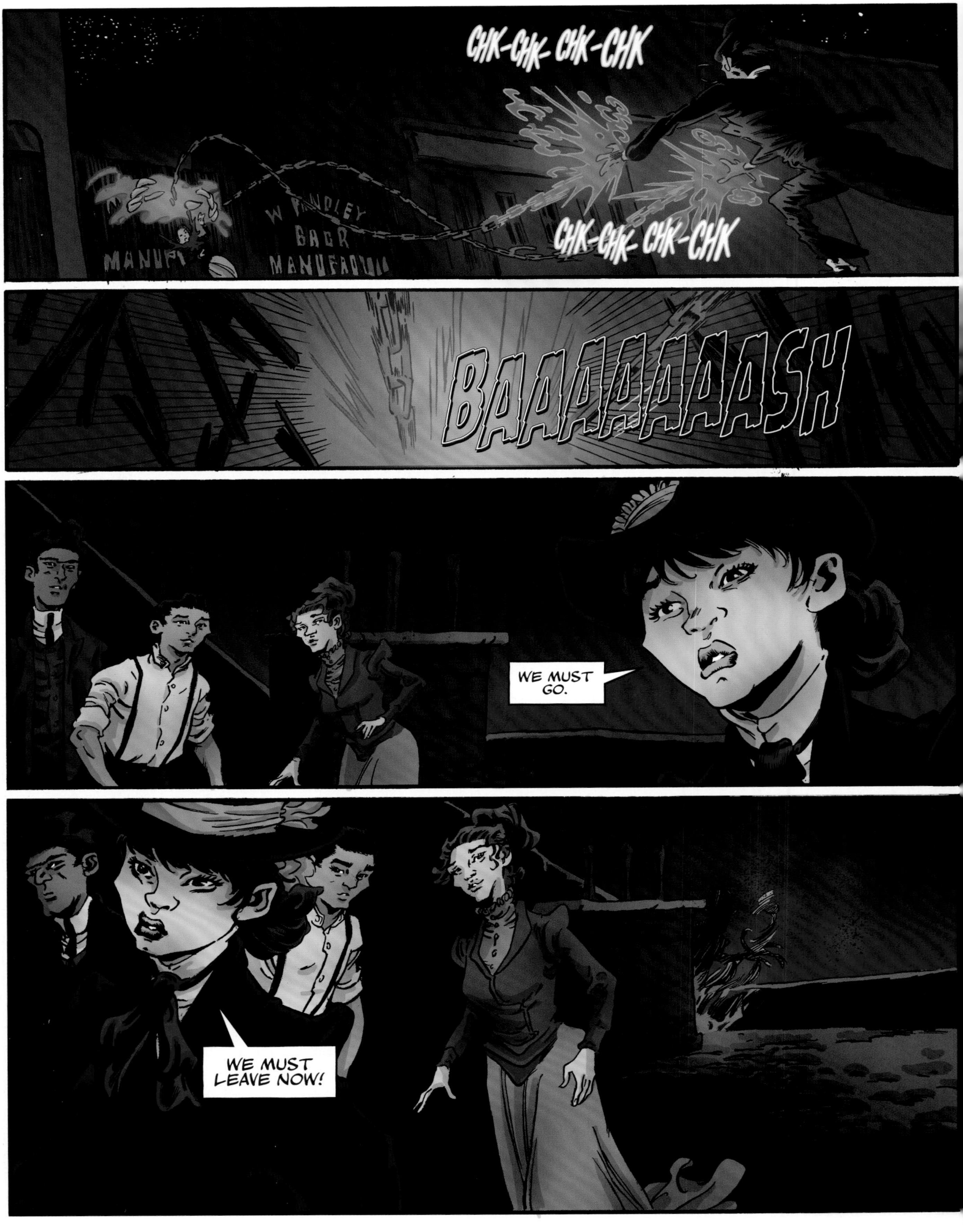
CHK-CHK- CHK-CHK
CHK-CHK- CHK-CHK
BAAAAAAASH
WE MUST GO.
WE MUST LEAVE NOW!

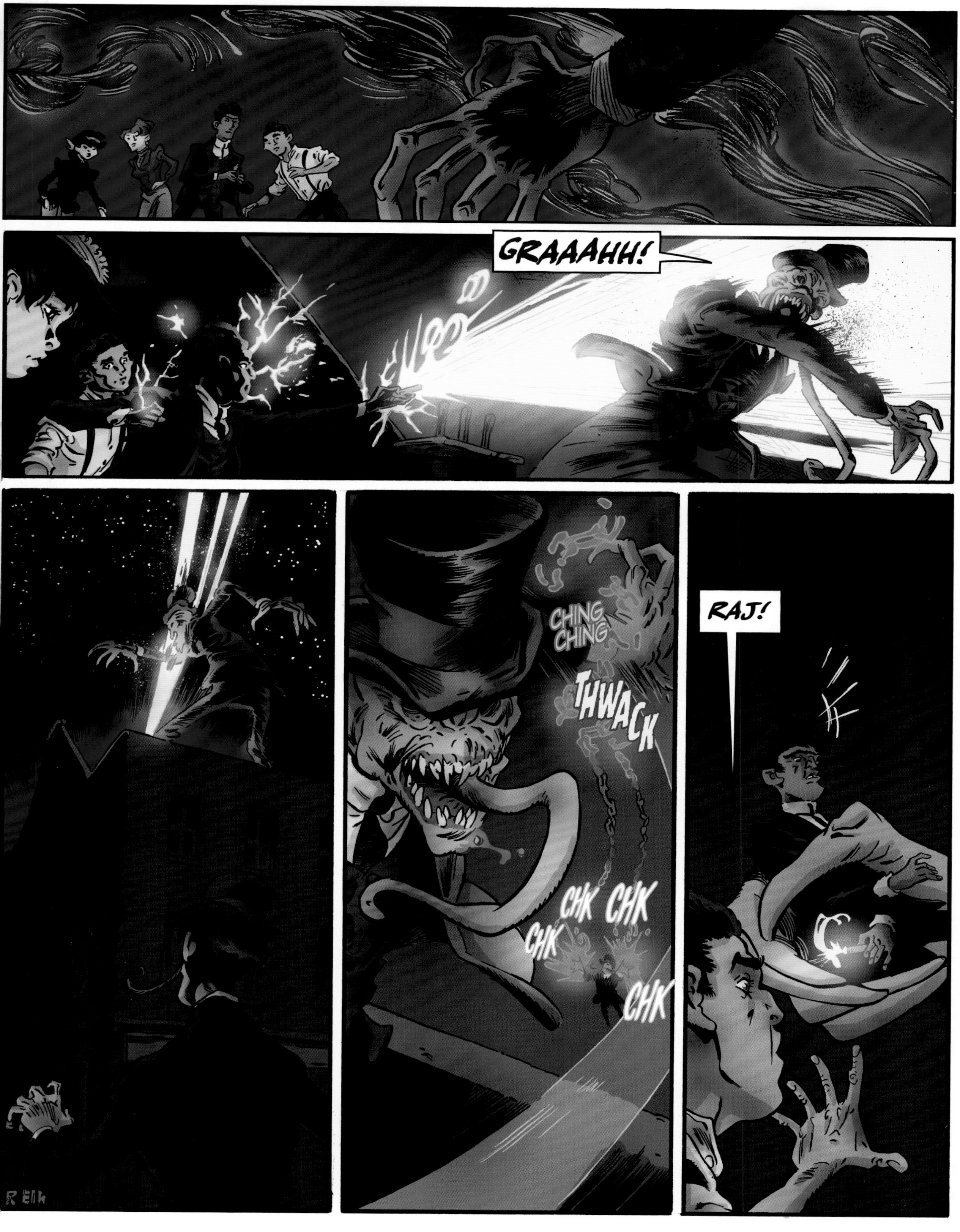
GRAAAHH!
CHING CHING
THWACK
CHK CHK
CHK
CHK
RAJ!
REIL

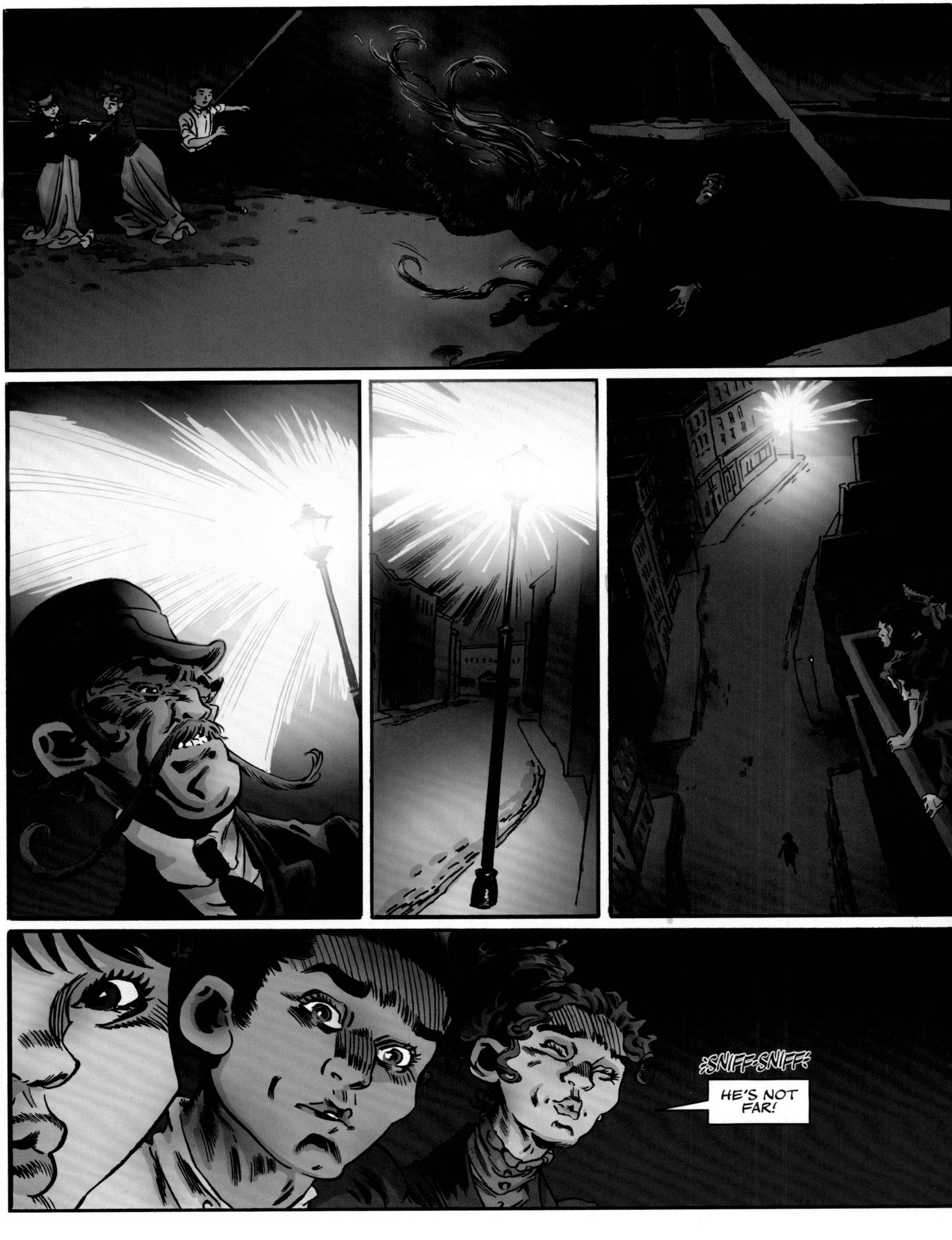
SNIFF SNIFF
HE'S NOT FAR!

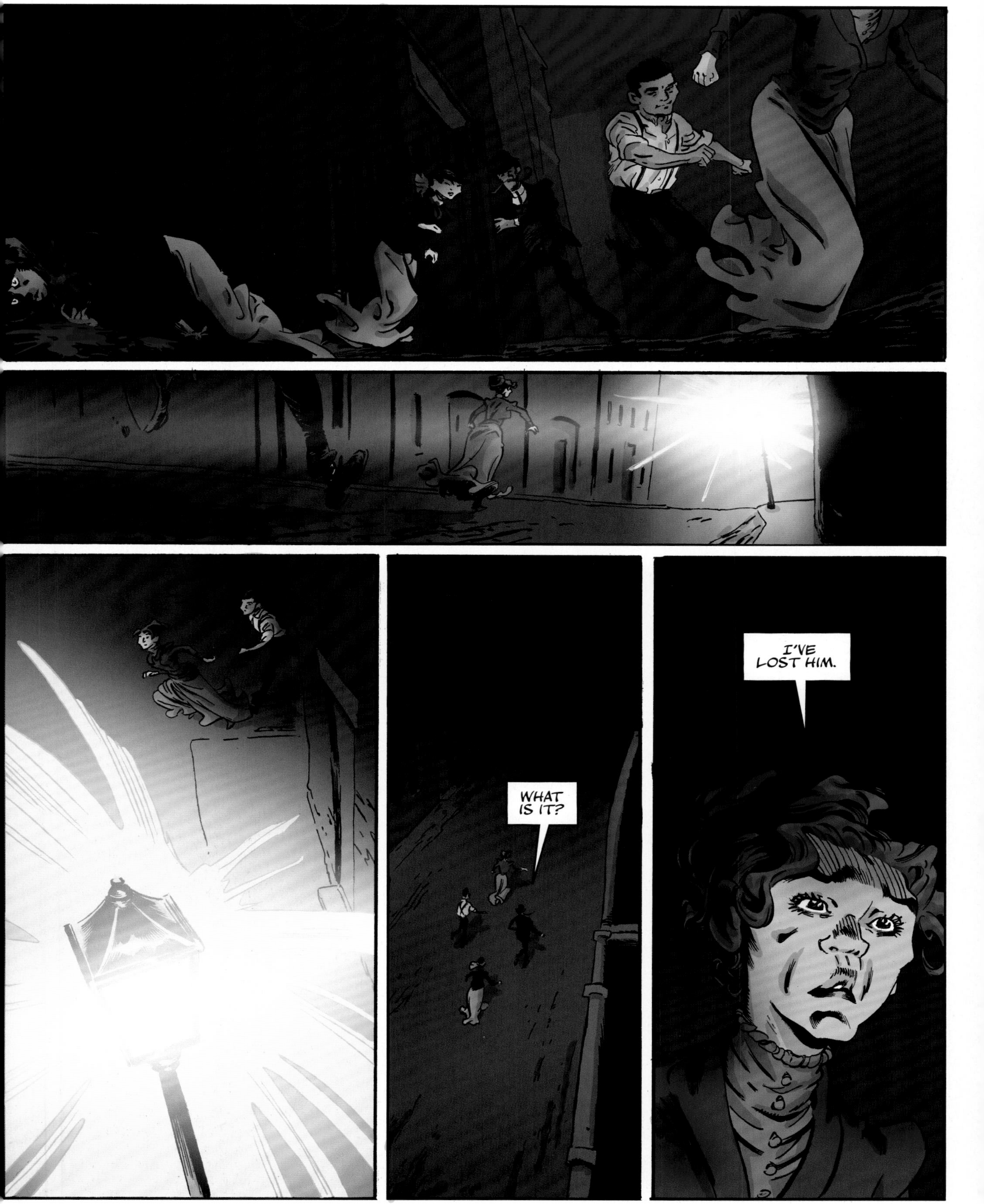
WHAT IS IT?
I'VE LOST HIM.

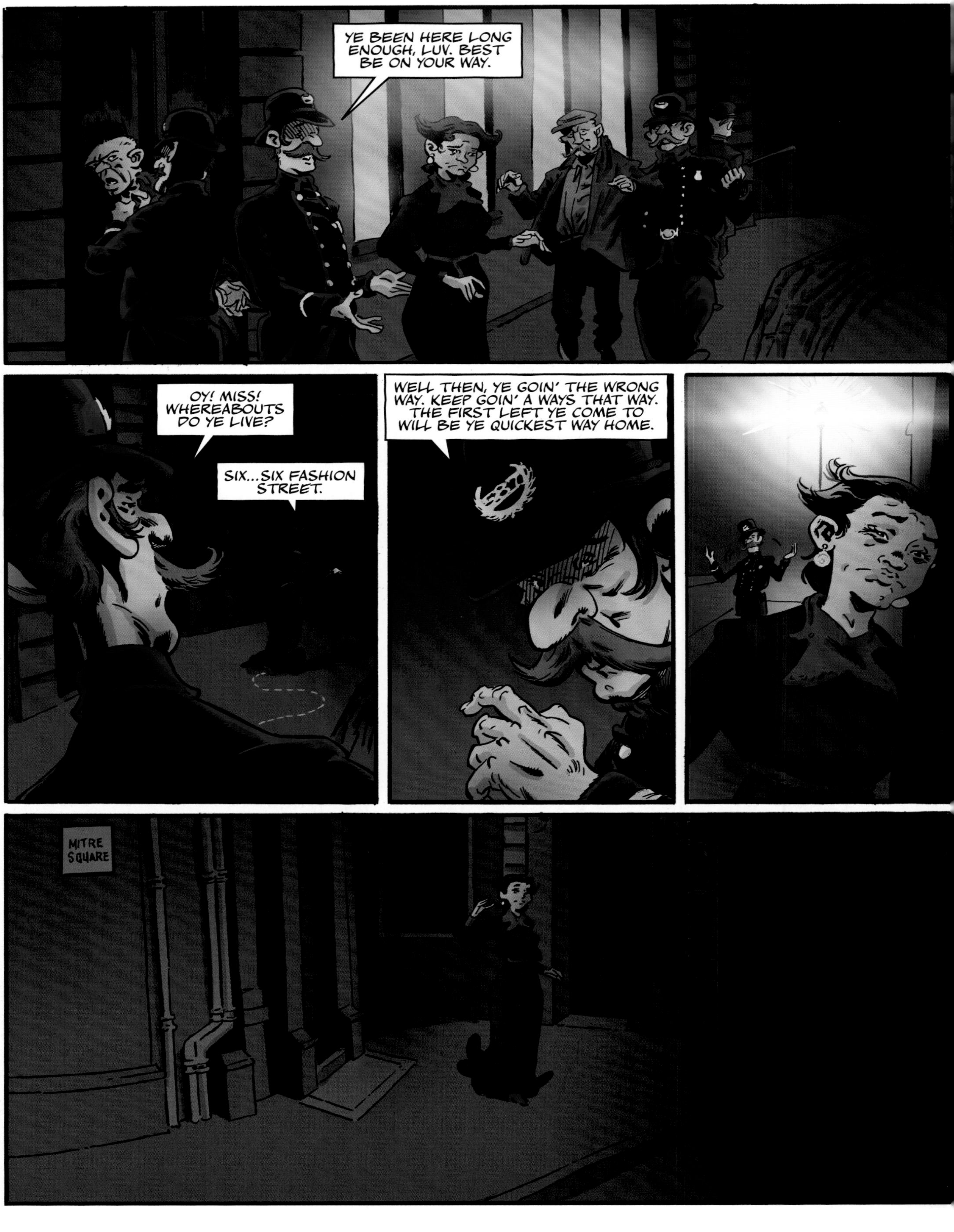
YE BEEN HERE LONG ENOUGH, LUV. BEST BE ON YOUR WAY.
OY! MISS! WHEREABOUTS DO YE LIVE?
SIX...SIX FASHION STREET.
WELL THEN, YE GOIN' THE WRONG WAY. KEEP GOIN' A WAYS THAT WAY. THE FIRST LEFT YE COME TO WILL BE YE QUICKEST WAY HOME.
MITRE SQUARE

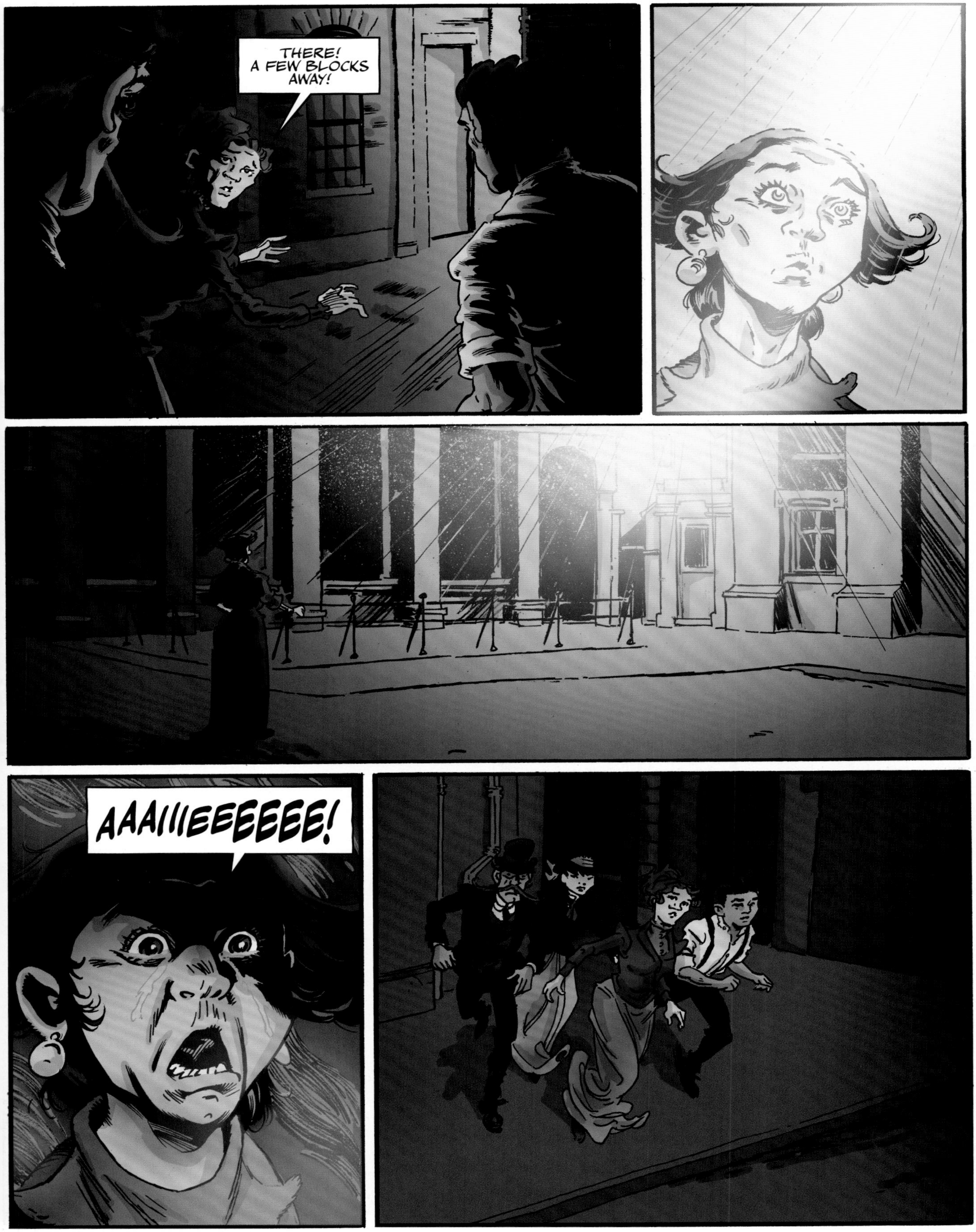
THERE! A FEW BLOCKS AWAY!
AAAIIIEEEEEEE!

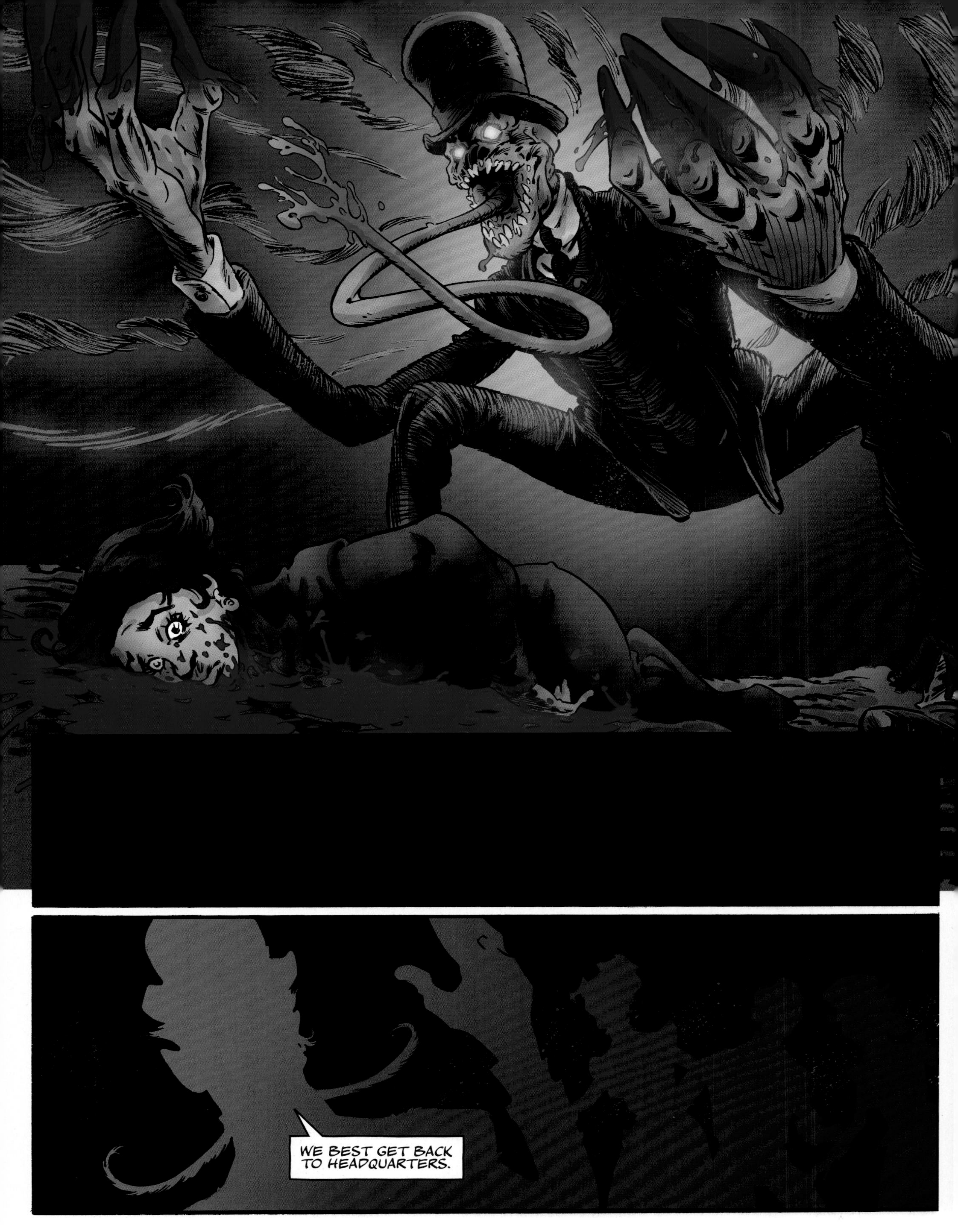
WE BEST GET BACK TO HEADQUARTERS.

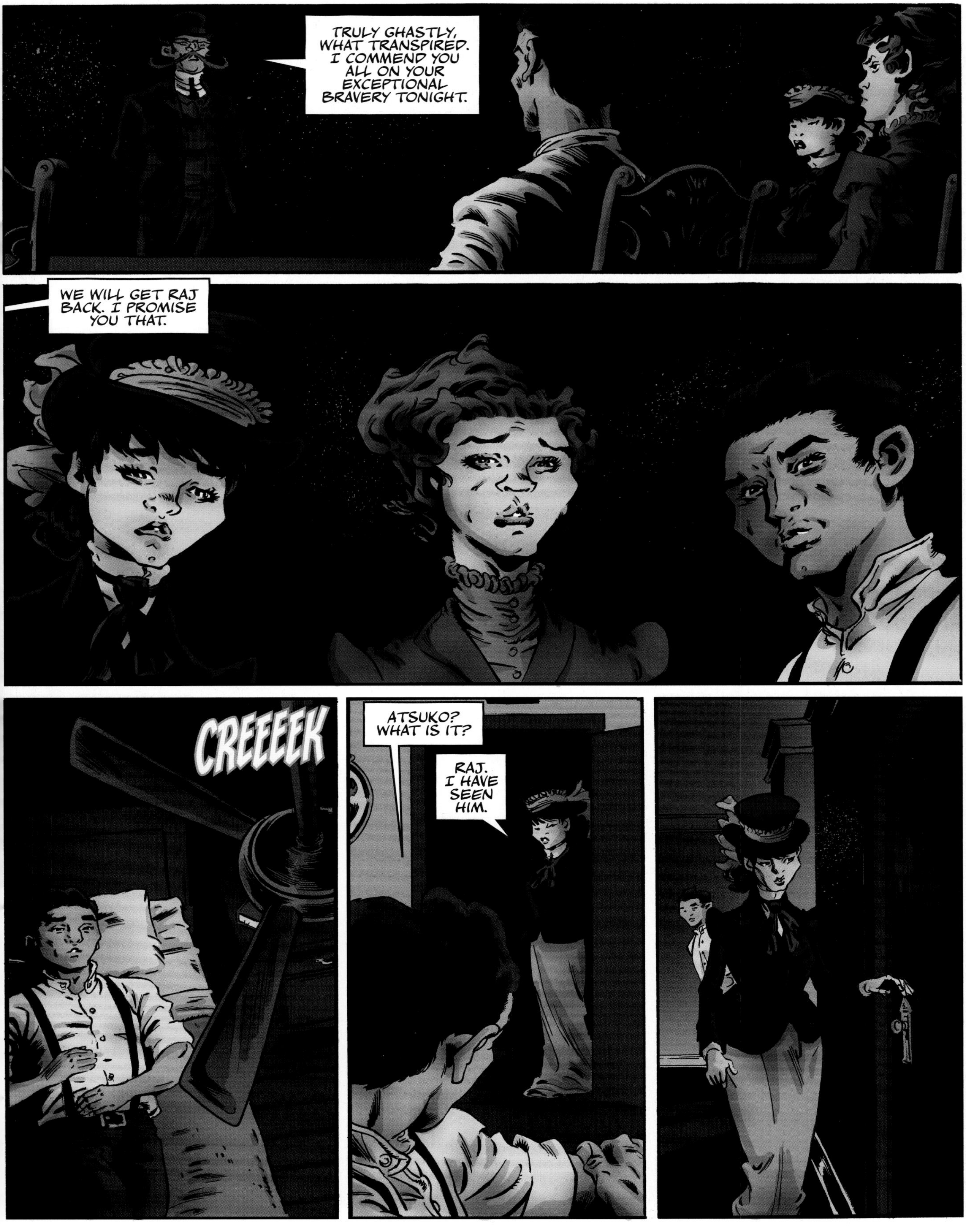
TRULY GHASTLY, WHAT TRANSPIRED. I COMMEND YOU ALL ON YOUR EXCEPTIONAL BRAVERY TONIGHT.
WE WILL GET RAJ BACK. I PROMISE YOU THAT.
CREEEEK
ATSUKO? WHAT IS IT?
RAJ. I HAVE SEEN HIM.

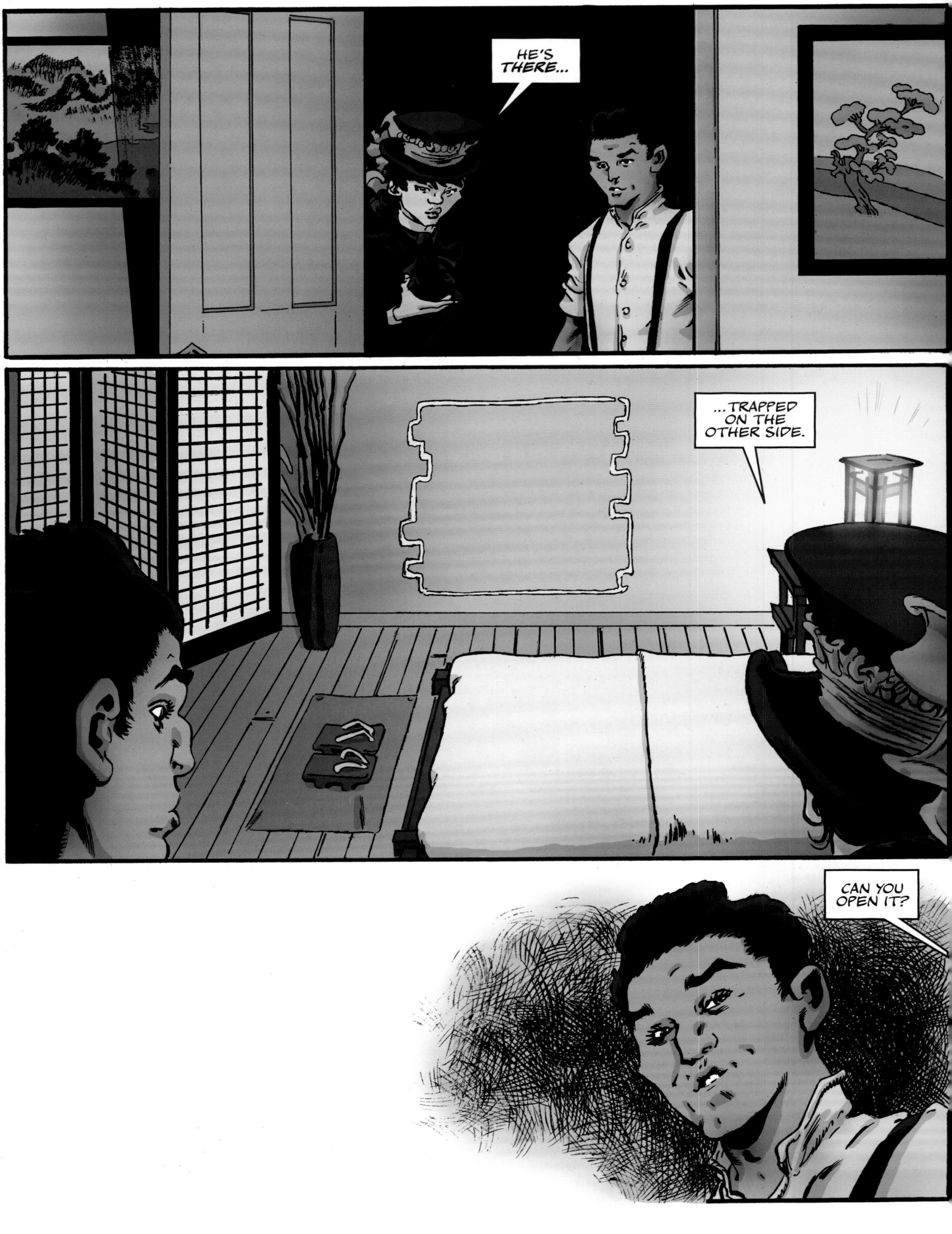
HE'S THERE...
...TRAPPED ON THE OTHER SIDE.
CAN YOU OPEN IT?

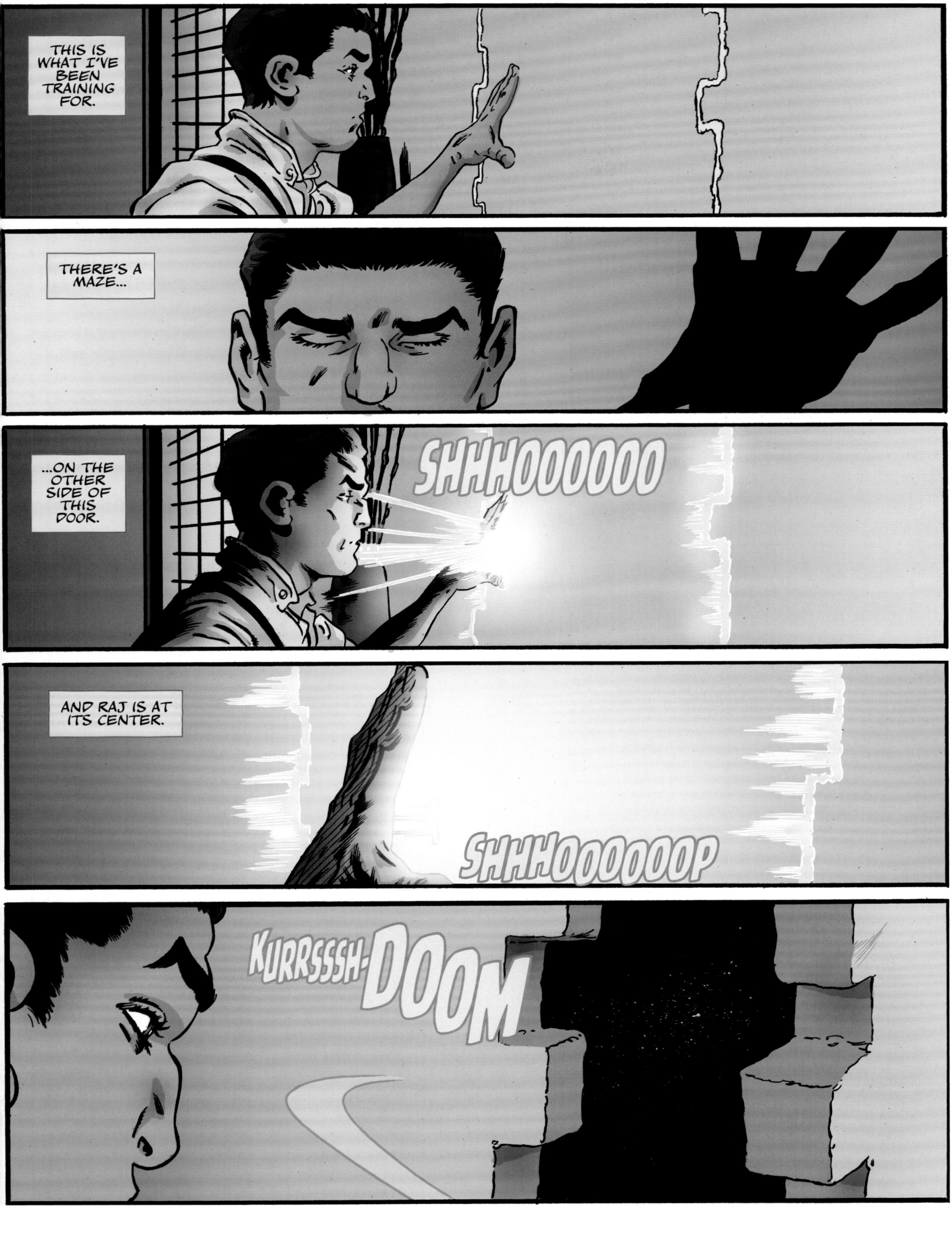
THIS IS WHAT I'VE BEEN TRAINING FOR.
THERE'S A MAZE...
...ON THE OTHER SIDE OF THIS DOOR.
SHHHOOOOOOO
AND RAJ IS AT ITS CENTER.
SHHHOOOOOOOP
KURRSSSH-DOOM

YOU'RE NOT COMING?

I CAN'T.

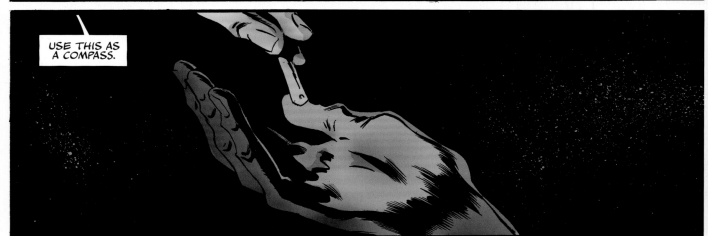

USE THIS AS A COMPASS.

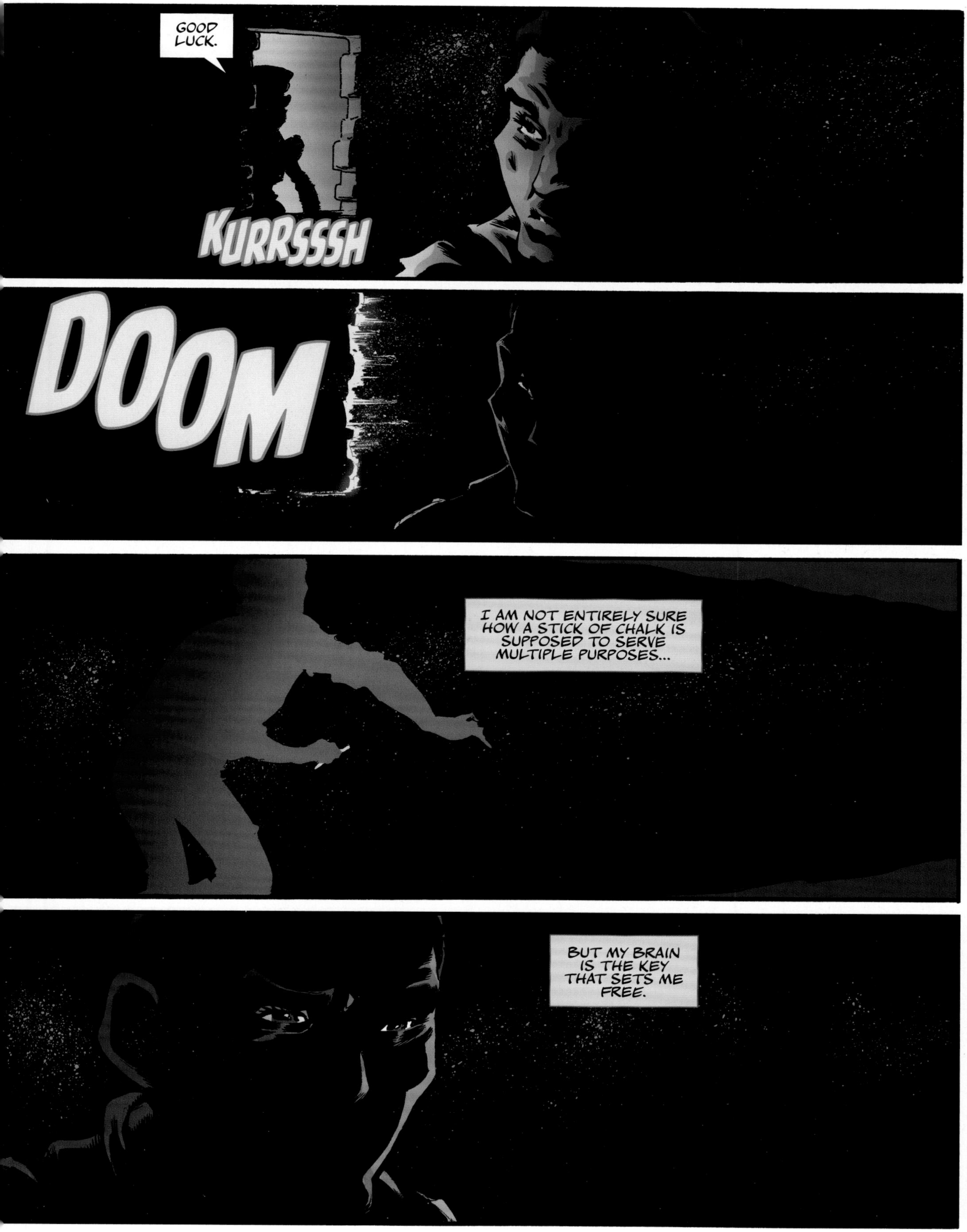
GOOD LUCK.
KURRSSSH
DOOM
I AM NOT ENTIRELY SURE HOW A STICK OF CHALK IS SUPPOSED TO SERVE MULTIPLE PURPOSES...
BUT MY BRAIN IS THE KEY THAT SETS ME FREE.

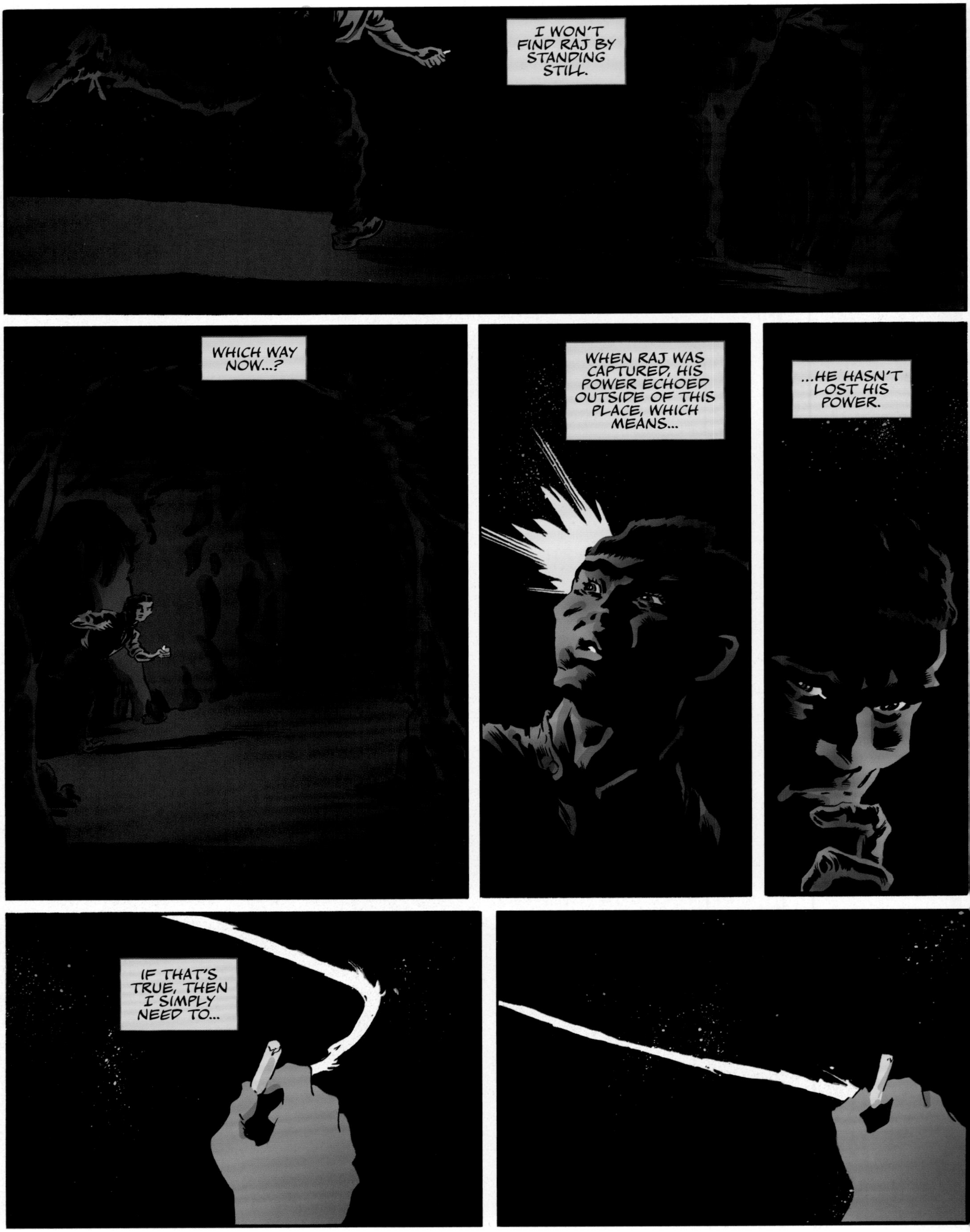
I WON'T FIND RAJ BY STANDING STILL.
WHICH WAY NOW...?
WHEN RAJ WAS CAPTURED, HIS POWER ECHOED OUTSIDE OF THIS PLACE, WHICH MEANS...
...HE HASN'T LOST HIS POWER.
IF THAT'S TRUE, THEN I SIMPLY NEED TO...

...FOLLOW HIS LIGHT!
HANG IN THERE, RAJ.
I'M ON MY WAY.

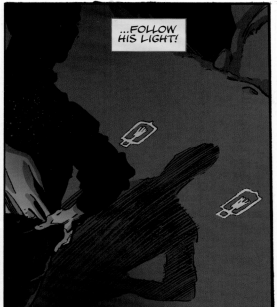

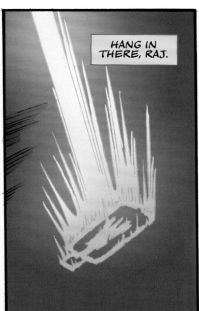

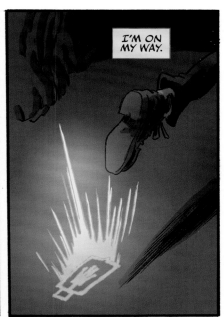

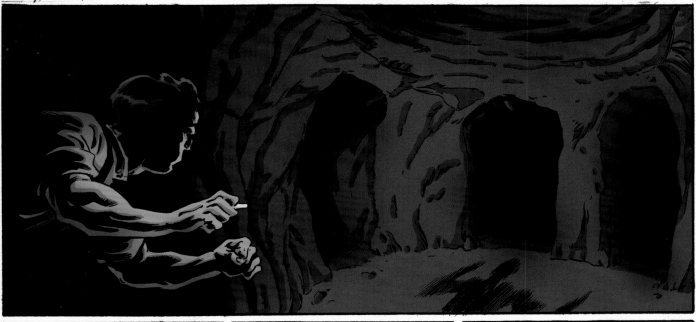

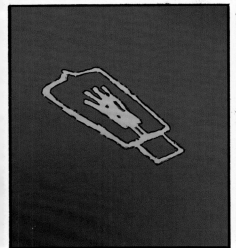

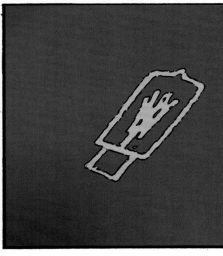

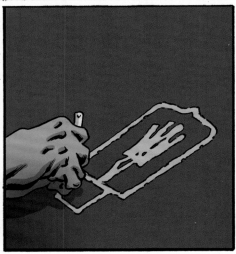

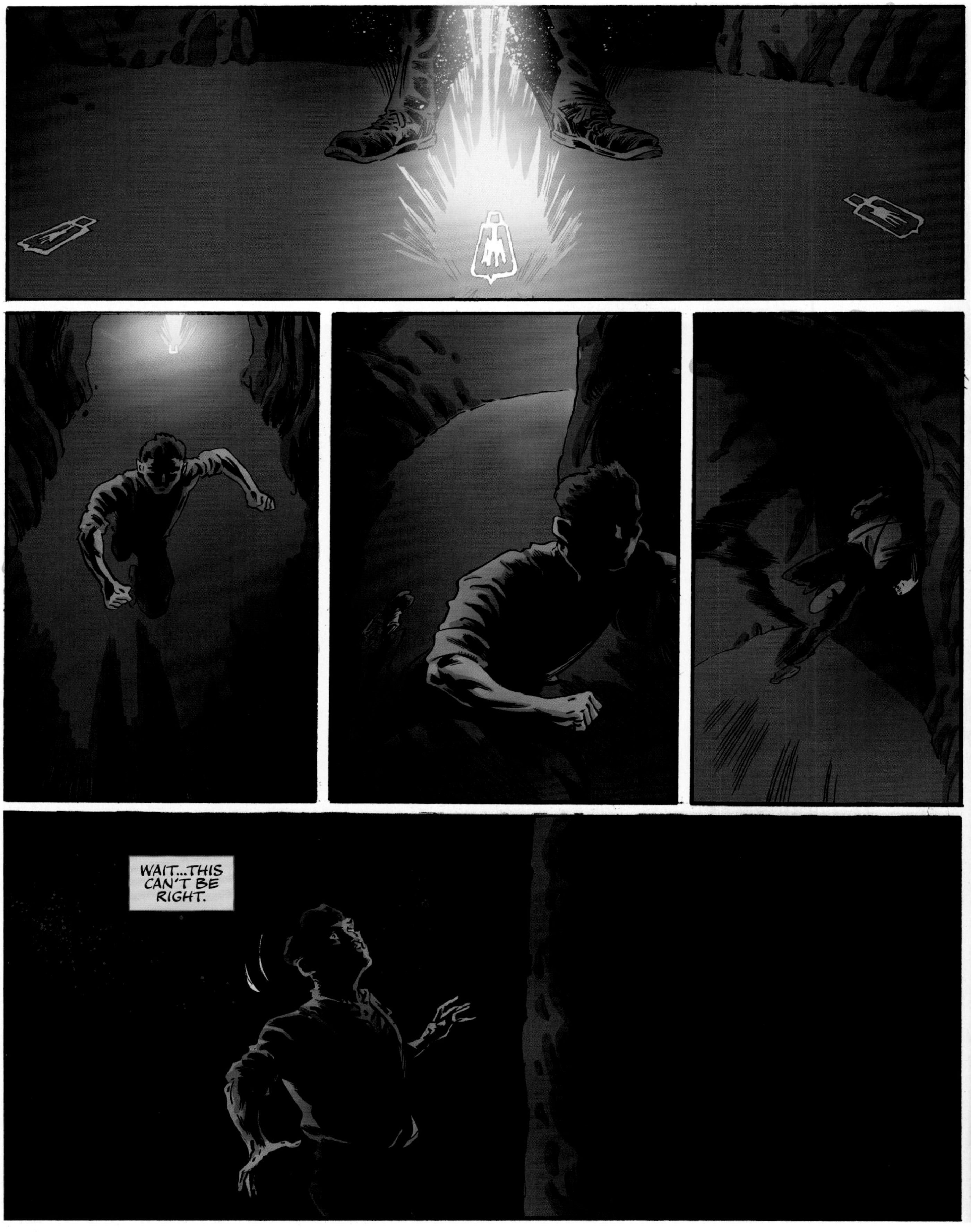
WAIT...THIS CAN'T BE RIGHT.

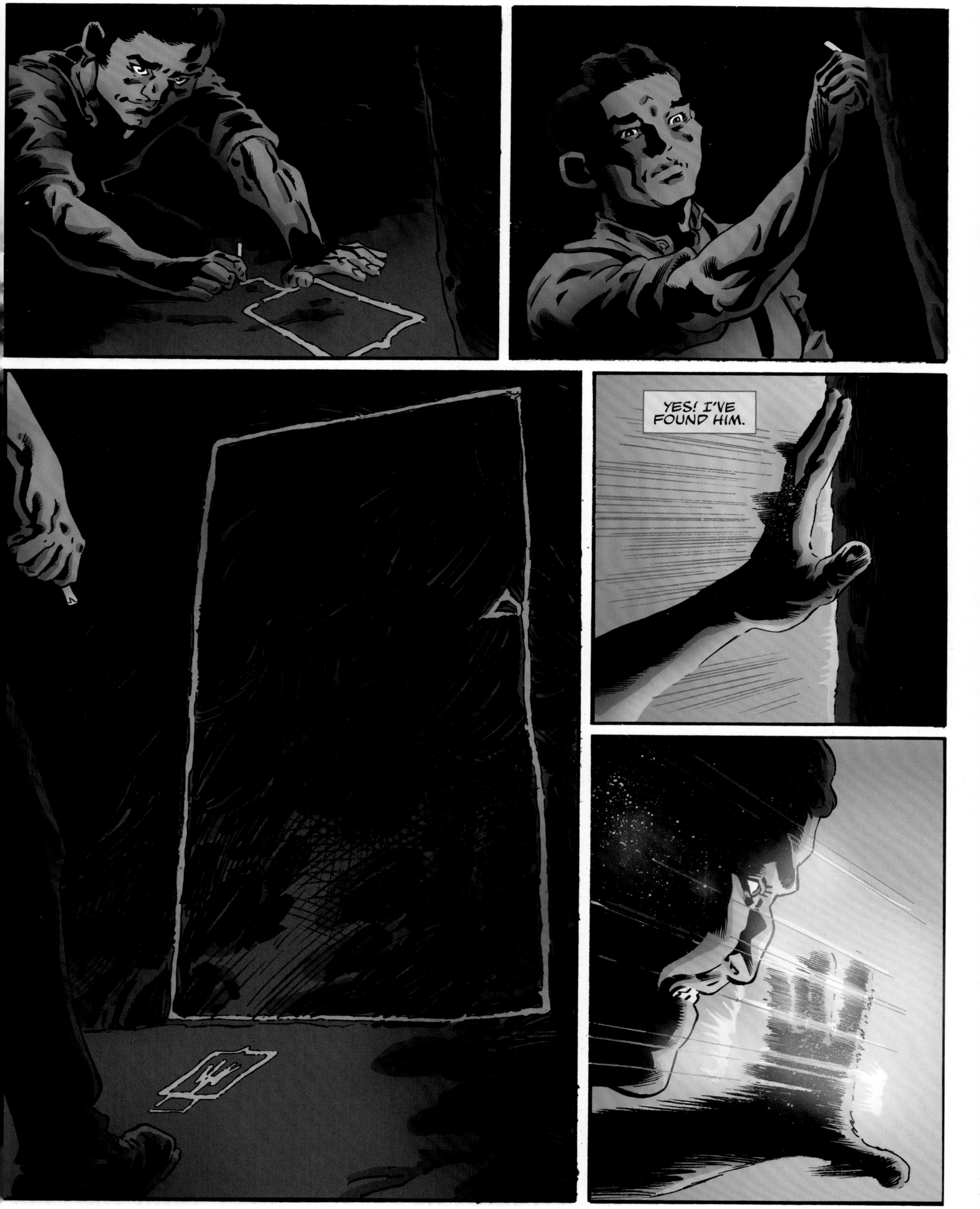
YES! I'VE FOUND HIM.

EHRICH? IS THAT YOU?
IT IS YOU! I'M SO HAPPY--
LET'S CELEBRATE LATER. FOLLOW ME.
WHO ARE YOU?

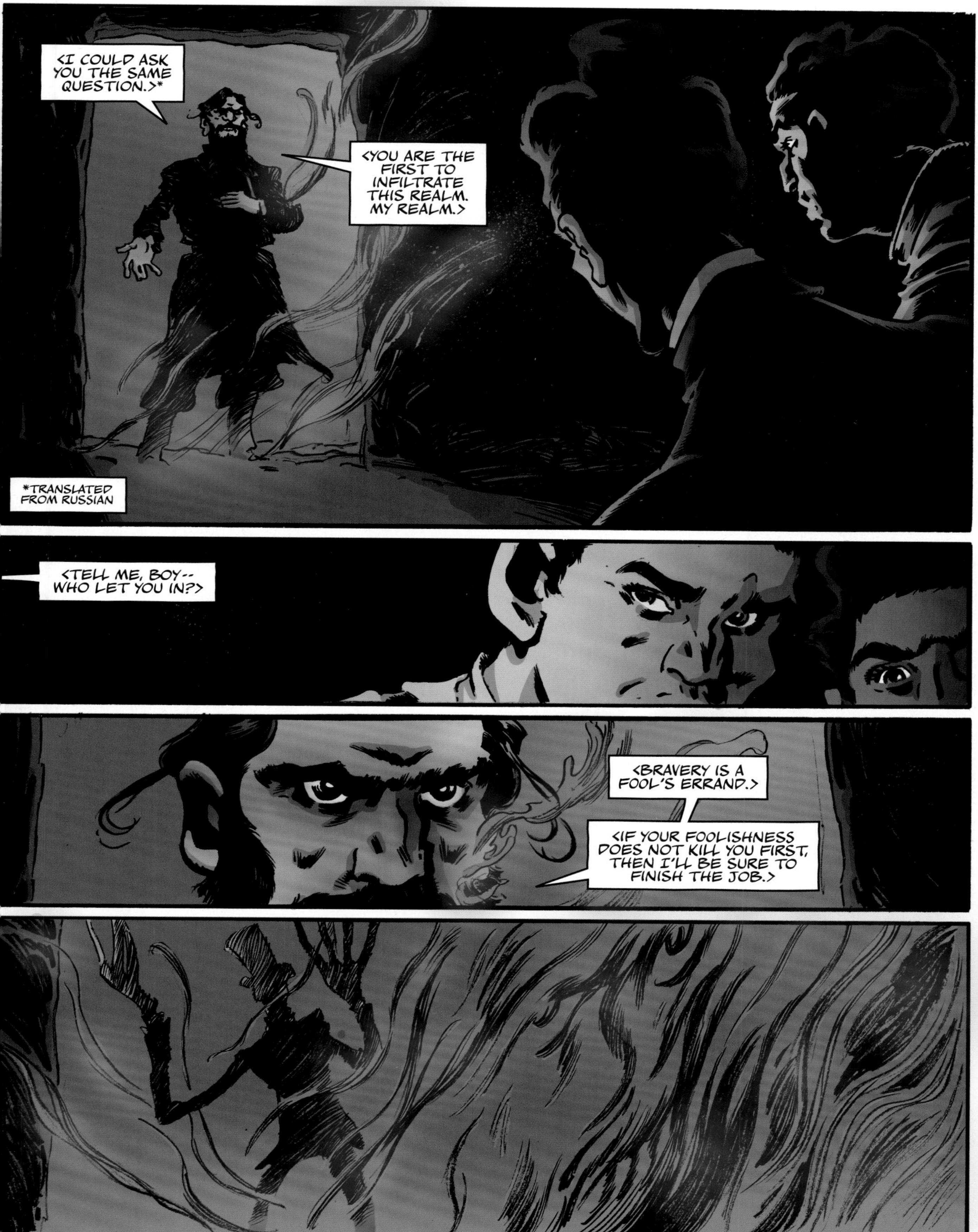
<I COULD ASK YOU THE SAME QUESTION.>*
<YOU ARE THE FIRST TO INFILTRATE THIS REALM. MY REALM.>
*TRANSLATED FROM RUSSIAN
<TELL ME, BOY-- WHO LET YOU IN?>
<BRAVERY IS A FOOL'S ERRAND.>
<IF YOUR FOOLISHNESS DOES NOT KILL YOU FIRST, THEN I'LL BE SURE TO FINISH THE JOB.>

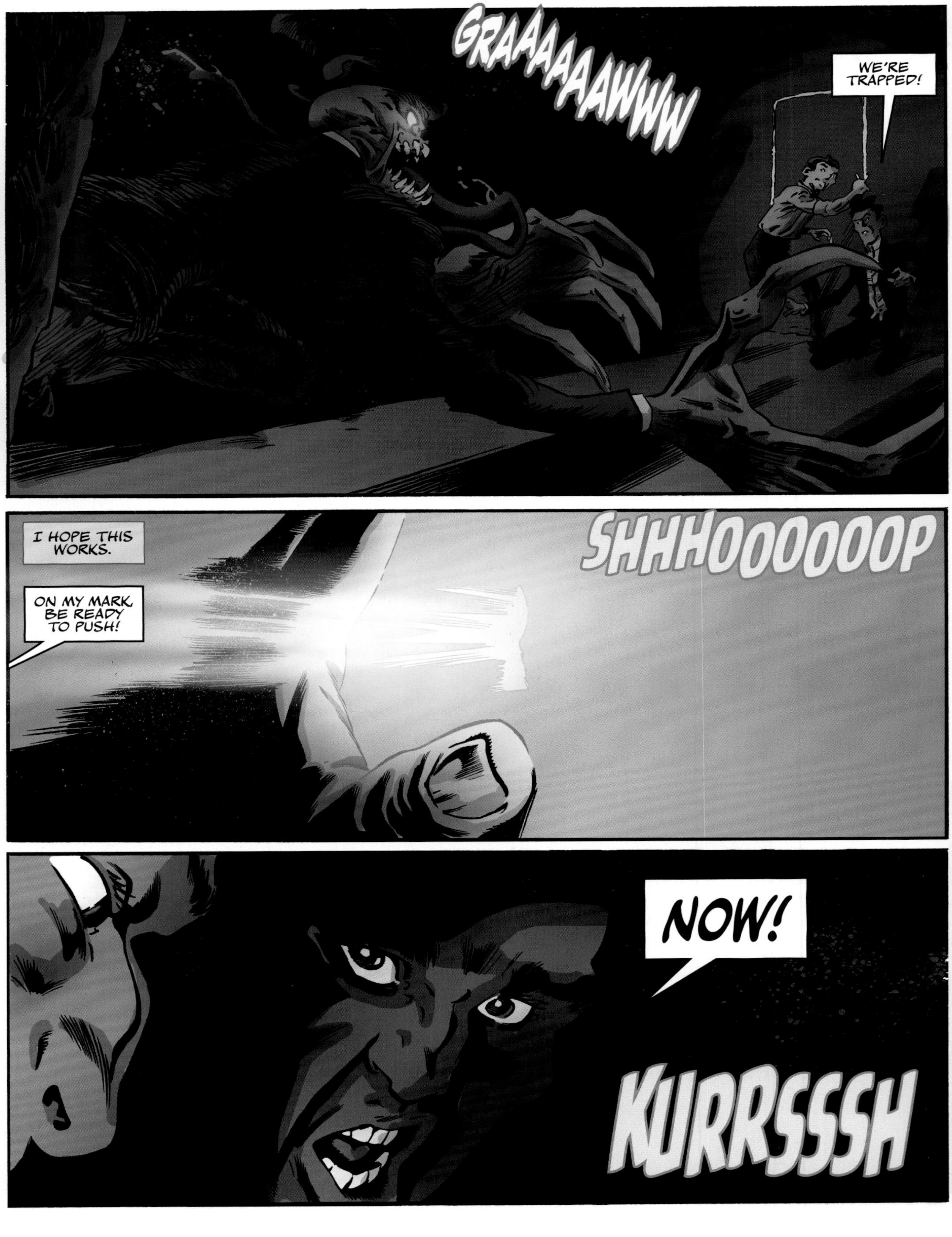
GRAAAAAAWWW
WE'RE TRAPPED!
I HOPE THIS WORKS.
ON MY MARK, BE READY TO PUSH!
SHHHOOOOOOOP
NOW!
KURRSSSH

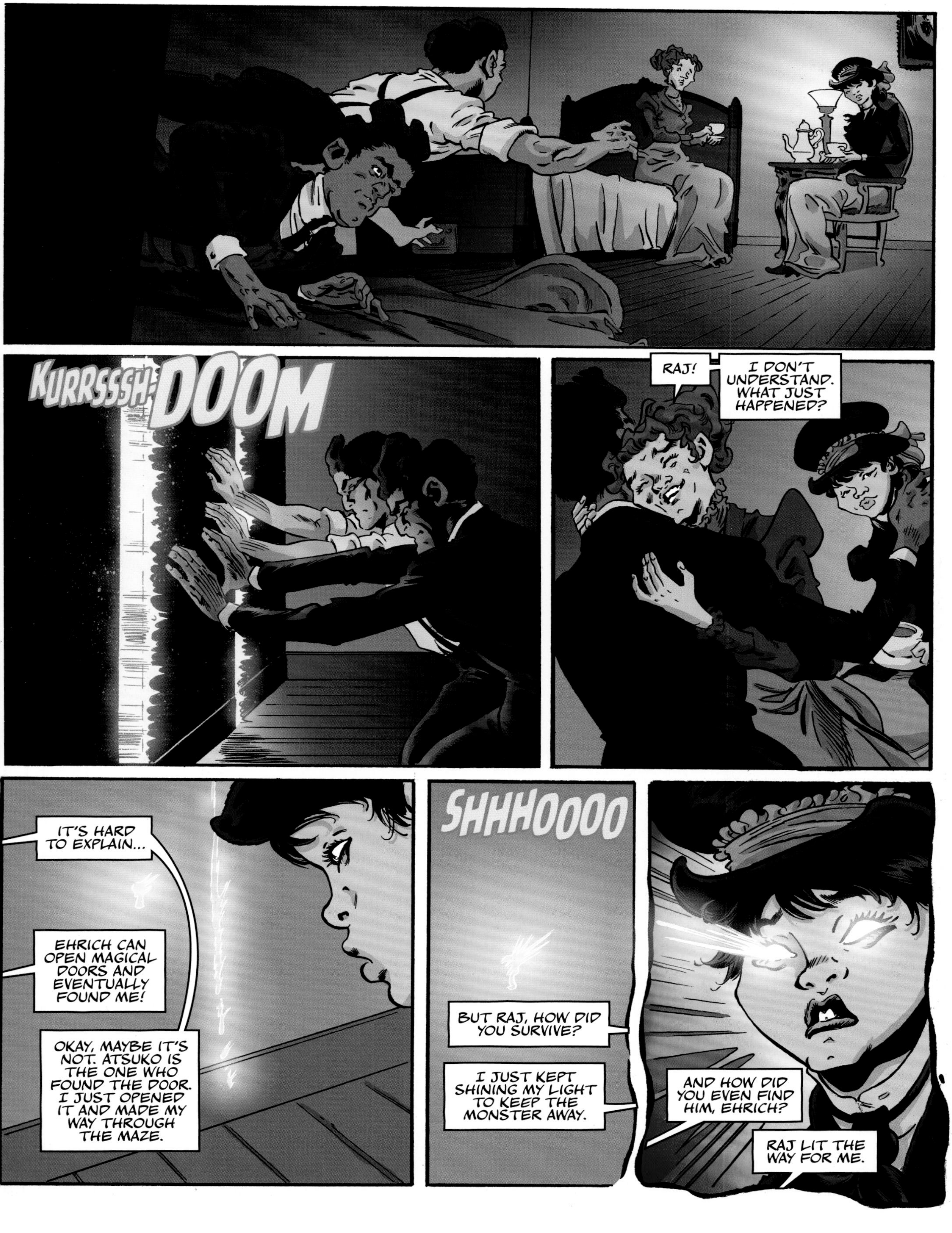
KURRSSSH-DOOM
RAJ!
I DON'T UNDERSTAND. WHAT JUST HAPPENED?
IT'S HARD TO EXPLAIN...
EHRICH CAN OPEN MAGICAL DOORS AND EVENTUALLY FOUND ME!
OKAY, MAYBE IT'S NOT. ATSUKO IS THE ONE WHO FOUND THE DOOR. I JUST OPENED IT AND MADE MY WAY THROUGH THE MAZE.
SHHHOOOO
BUT RAJ, HOW DID YOU SURVIVE?
I JUST KEPT SHINING MY LIGHT TO KEEP THE MONSTER AWAY.
AND HOW DID YOU EVEN FIND HIM, EHRICH?
RAJ LIT THE WAY FOR ME.

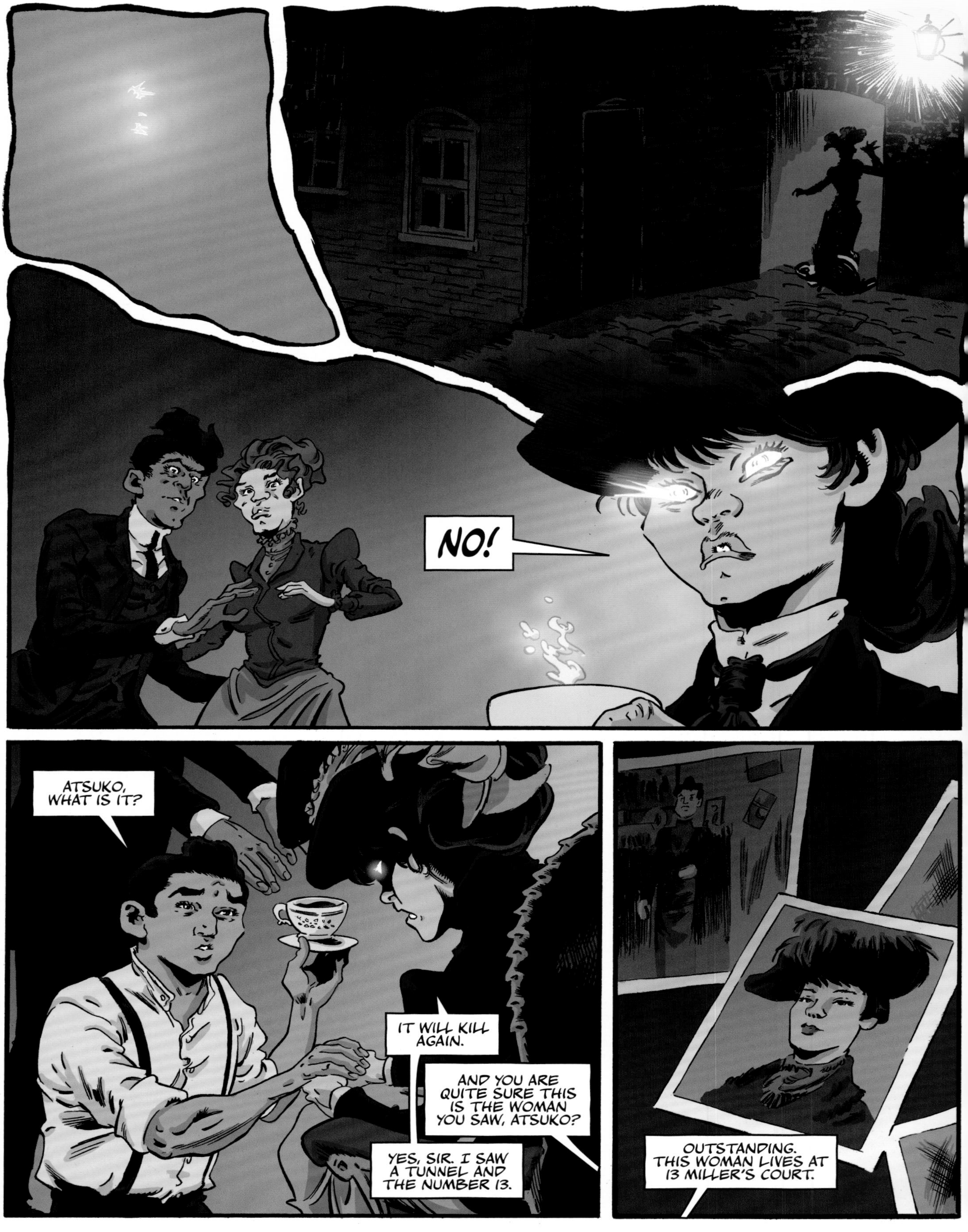
NO!
ATSUKO, WHAT IS IT?
IT WILL KILL AGAIN.
AND YOU ARE QUITE SURE THIS IS THE WOMAN YOU SAW, ATSUKO?
YES, SIR. I SAW A TUNNEL AND THE NUMBER 13.
OUTSTANDING. THIS WOMAN LIVES AT 13 MILLER'S COURT.

EXCELLENT WORK. ALL OF YOU. WE MAY INTERCEPT THIS MONSTER ONCE AND FOR ALL.

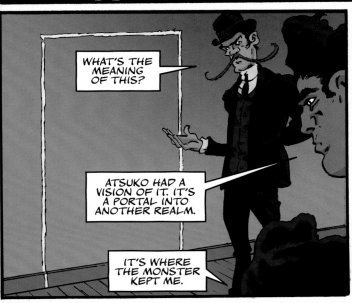

WHAT'S THE MEANING OF THIS?

ATSUKO HAD A VISION OF IT. IT'S A PORTAL INTO ANOTHER REALM.

IT'S WHERE THE MONSTER KEPT ME.

BUT WHAT ABOUT THE MAN WHO WAS THERE? WHO WAS HE?

THERE'S SOMETHING YOU ALL NEED TO SEE.

EVERYTHING WE'VE COME TO LEARN ABOUT THE BEAST HAS INFORMED US ON HOW BEST TO CONTAIN IT.

WHAT YOU'RE ABOUT TO SEE IS THE CULMINATION OF OUR COMBINED EFFORTS.

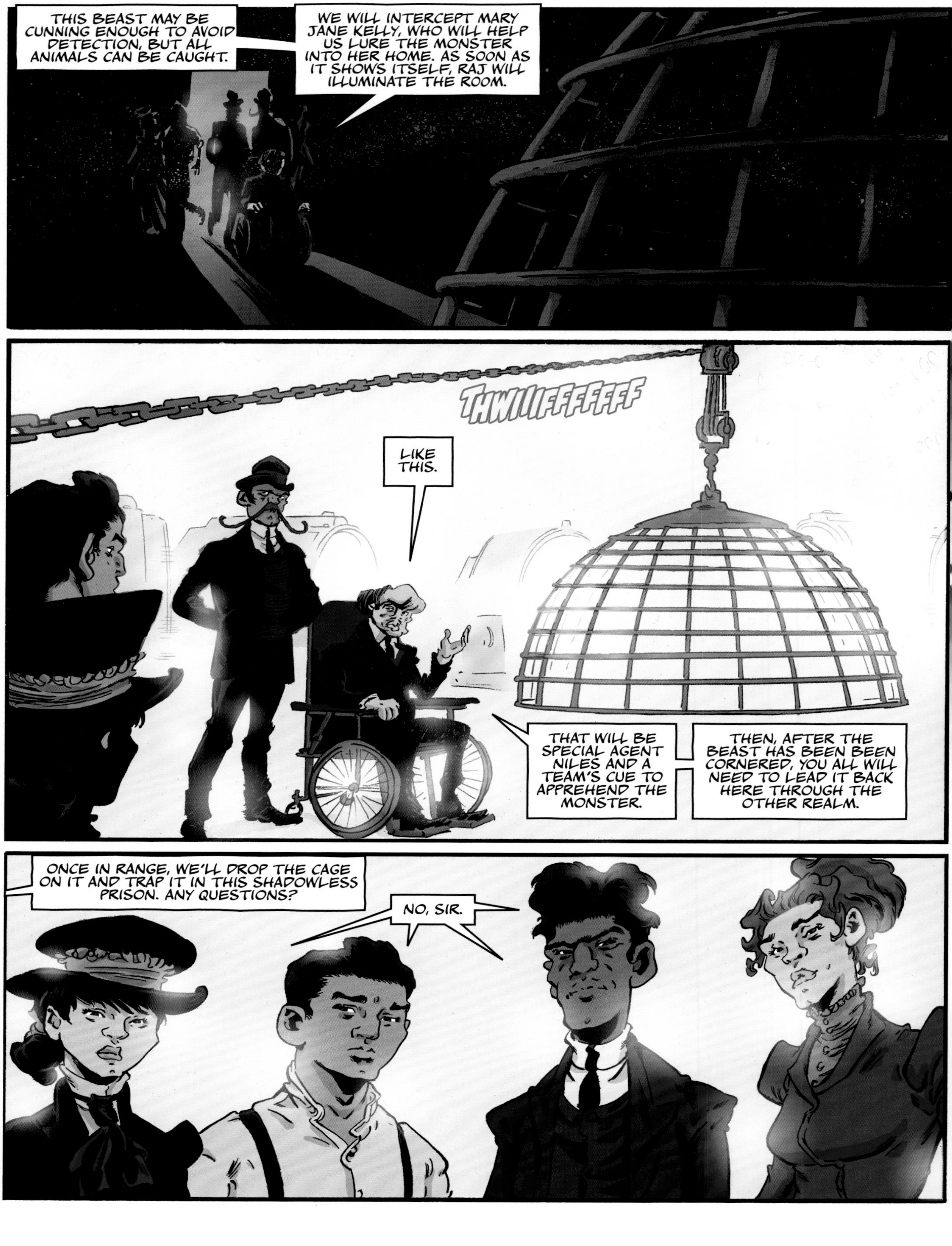
THIS BEAST MAY BE CUNNING ENOUGH TO AVOID DETECTION, BUT ALL ANIMALS CAN BE CAUGHT.
WE WILL INTERCEPT MARY JANE KELLY, WHO WILL HELP US LURE THE MONSTER INTO HER HOME. AS SOON AS IT SHOWS ITSELF, RAJ WILL ILLUMINATE THE ROOM.
THWIIIFFFFFF
LIKE THIS.
THAT WILL BE SPECIAL AGENT NILES AND A TEAM'S CUE TO APPREHEND THE MONSTER.
THEN, AFTER THE BEAST HAS BEEN BEEN CORNERED, YOU ALL WILL NEED TO LEAD IT BACK HERE THROUGH THE OTHER REALM.
ONCE IN RANGE, WE'LL DROP THE CAGE ON IT AND TRAP IT IN THIS SHADOWLESS PRISON. ANY QUESTIONS?
NO, SIR.

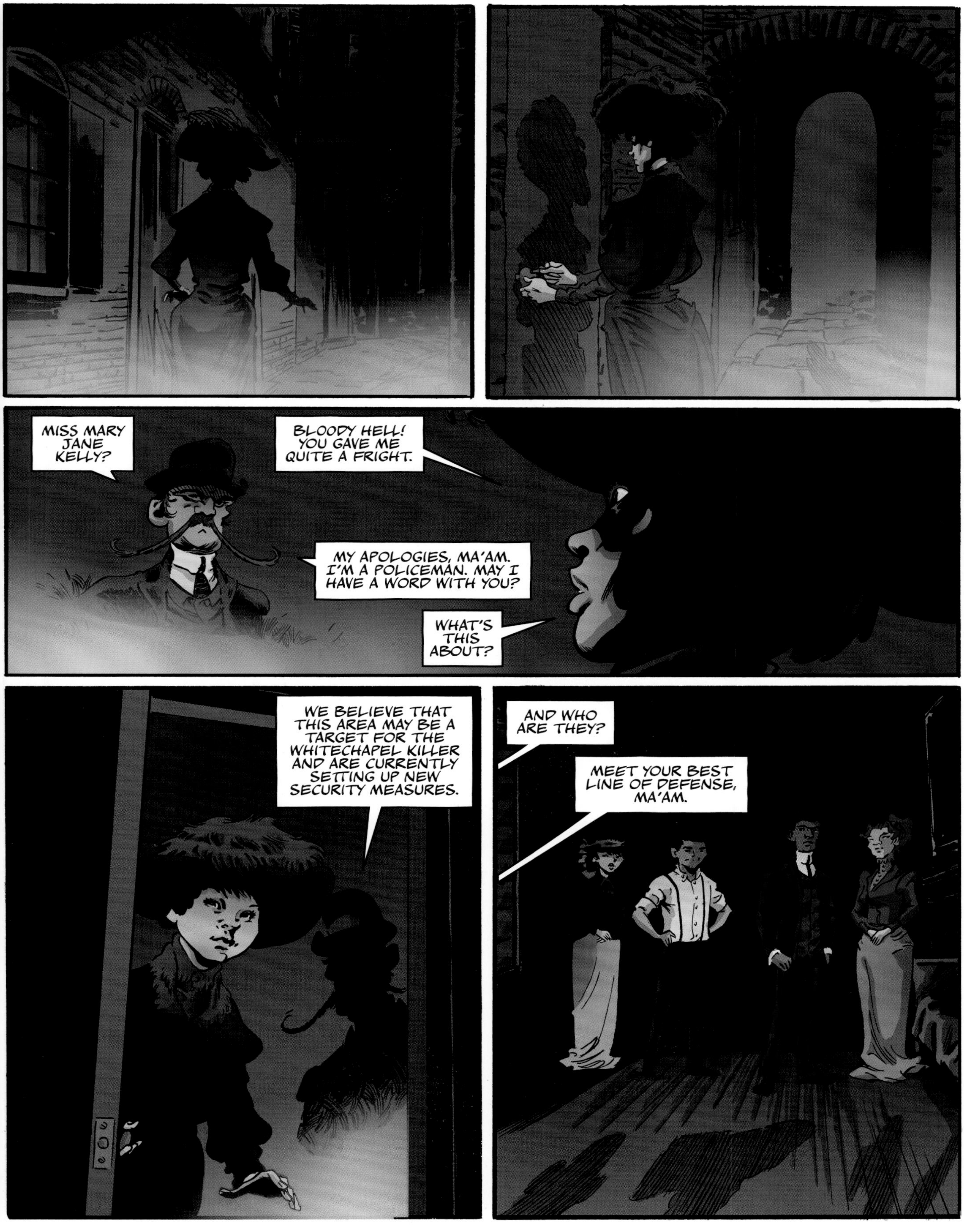

MISS MARY JANE KELLY?
BLOODY HELL! YOU GAVE ME QUITE A FRIGHT.
MY APOLOGIES, MA'AM. I'M A POLICEMAN. MAY I HAVE A WORD WITH YOU?
WHAT'S THIS ABOUT?
WE BELIEVE THAT THIS AREA MAY BE A TARGET FOR THE WHITECHAPEL KILLER AND ARE CURRENTLY SETTING UP NEW SECURITY MEASURES.
AND WHO ARE THEY?
MEET YOUR BEST LINE OF DEFENSE, MA'AM.

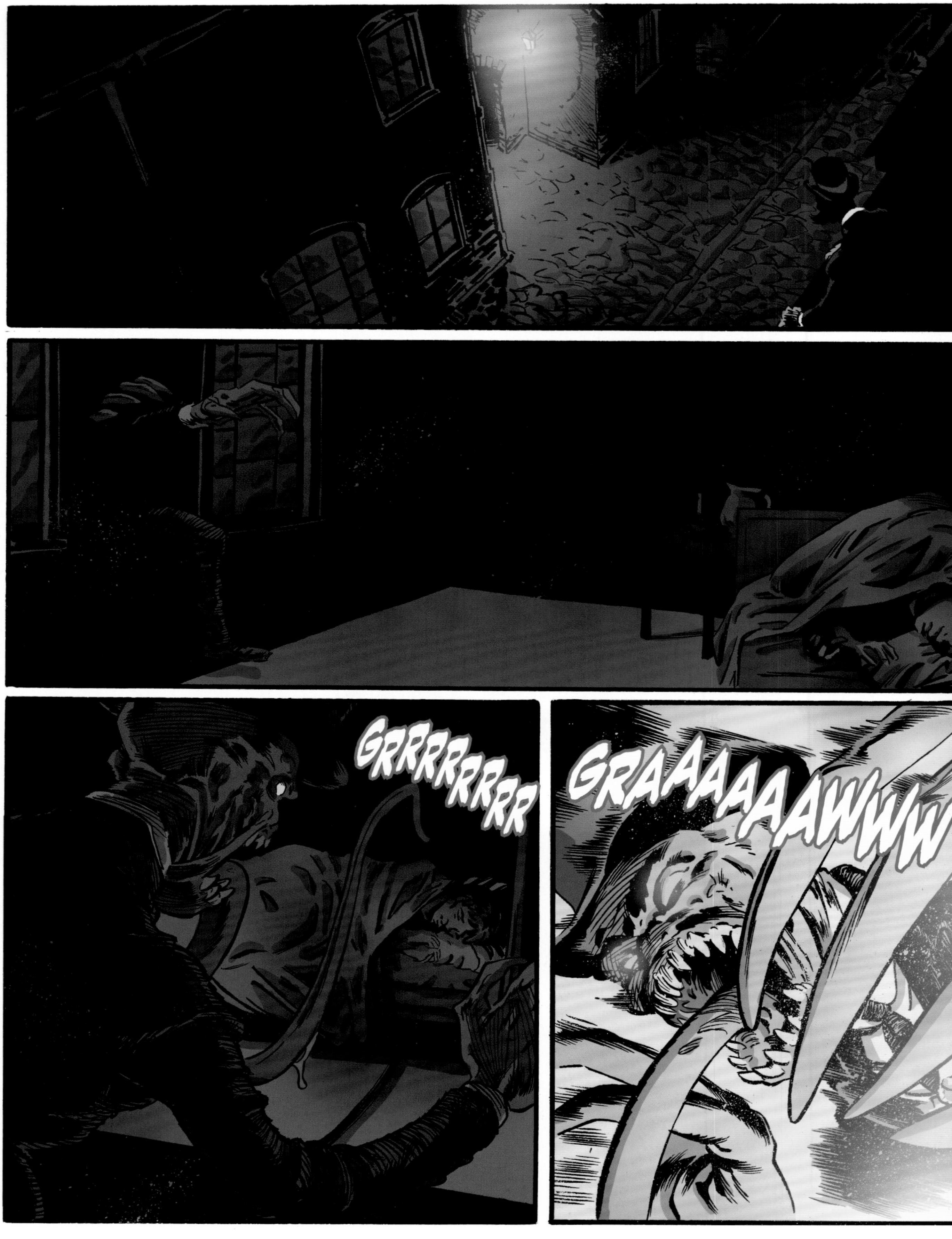
GRRRRRRRRR
GRAAAAAAAWWWW

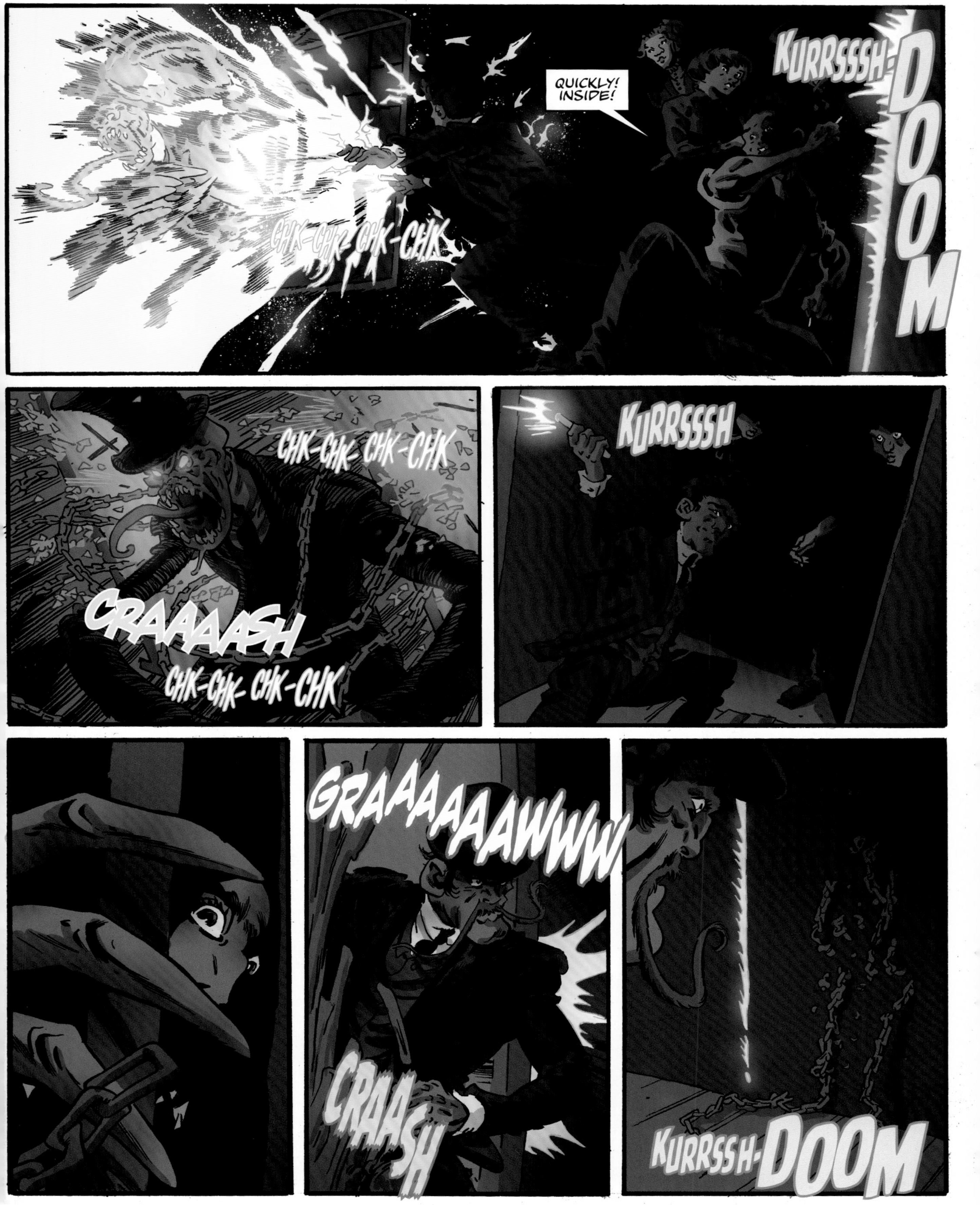
QUICKLY! INSIDE!
KURRSSSH-DOOOM
CHK-CHK-CHK-CHK
CHK-CHK-CHK-CHK
CRAAAASH
CHK-CHK-CHK-CHK
KURRSSSH
GRAAAAAAAWWW
CRAASH
KURRSSH-DOOM

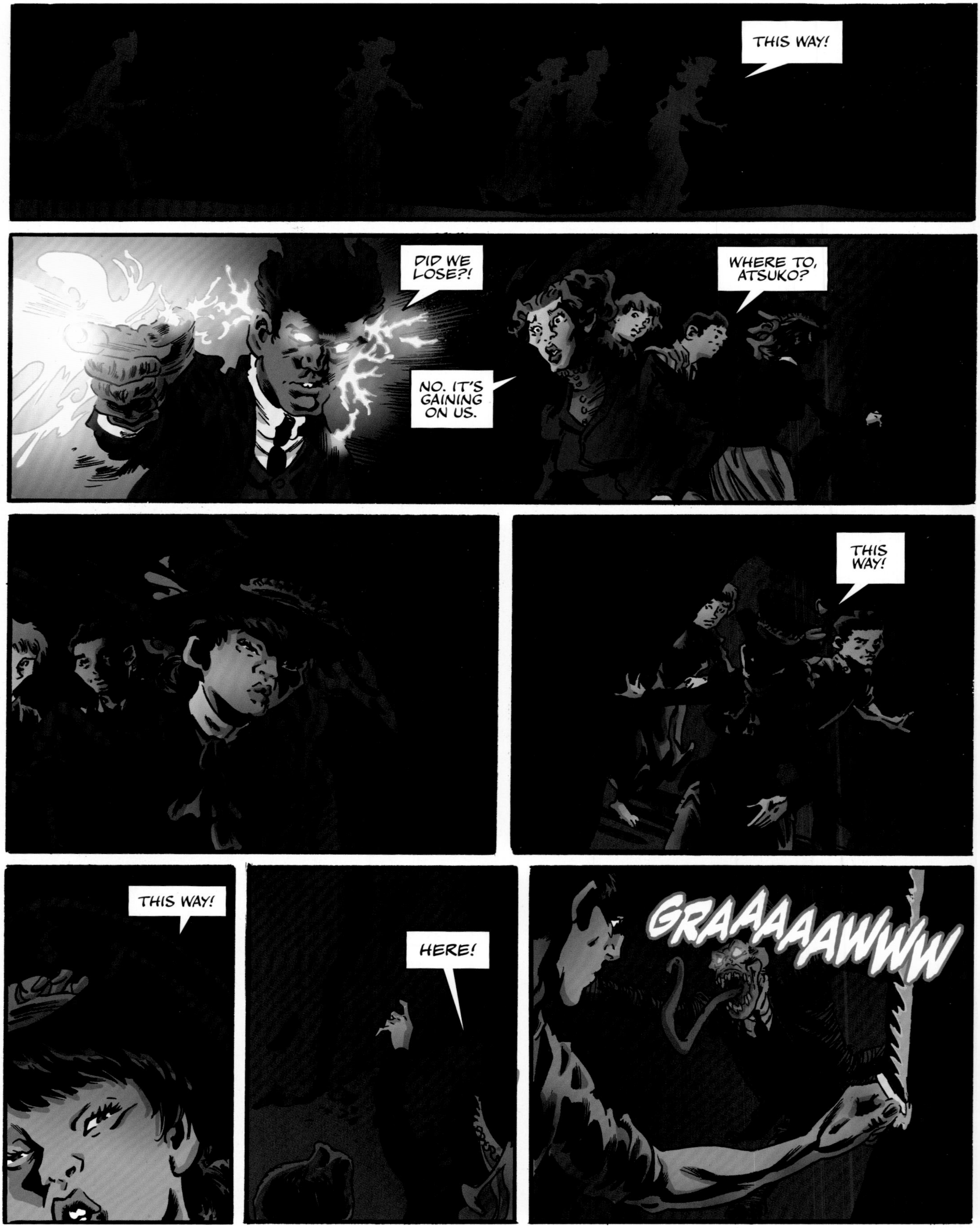
THIS WAY!
DID WE LOSE?!
NO. IT'S GAINING ON US.
WHERE TO, ATSUKO?
THIS WAY!
THIS WAY!
HERE!
GRAAAAAAWWW

SHHHOOOOOO

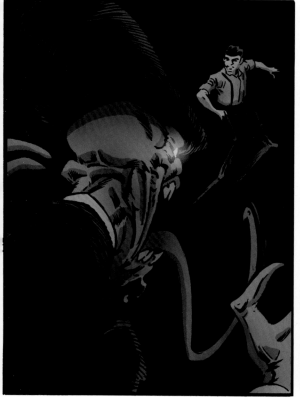

CHUNK
CHUNK
CHUNK
CHUNK

BOOOOOOM

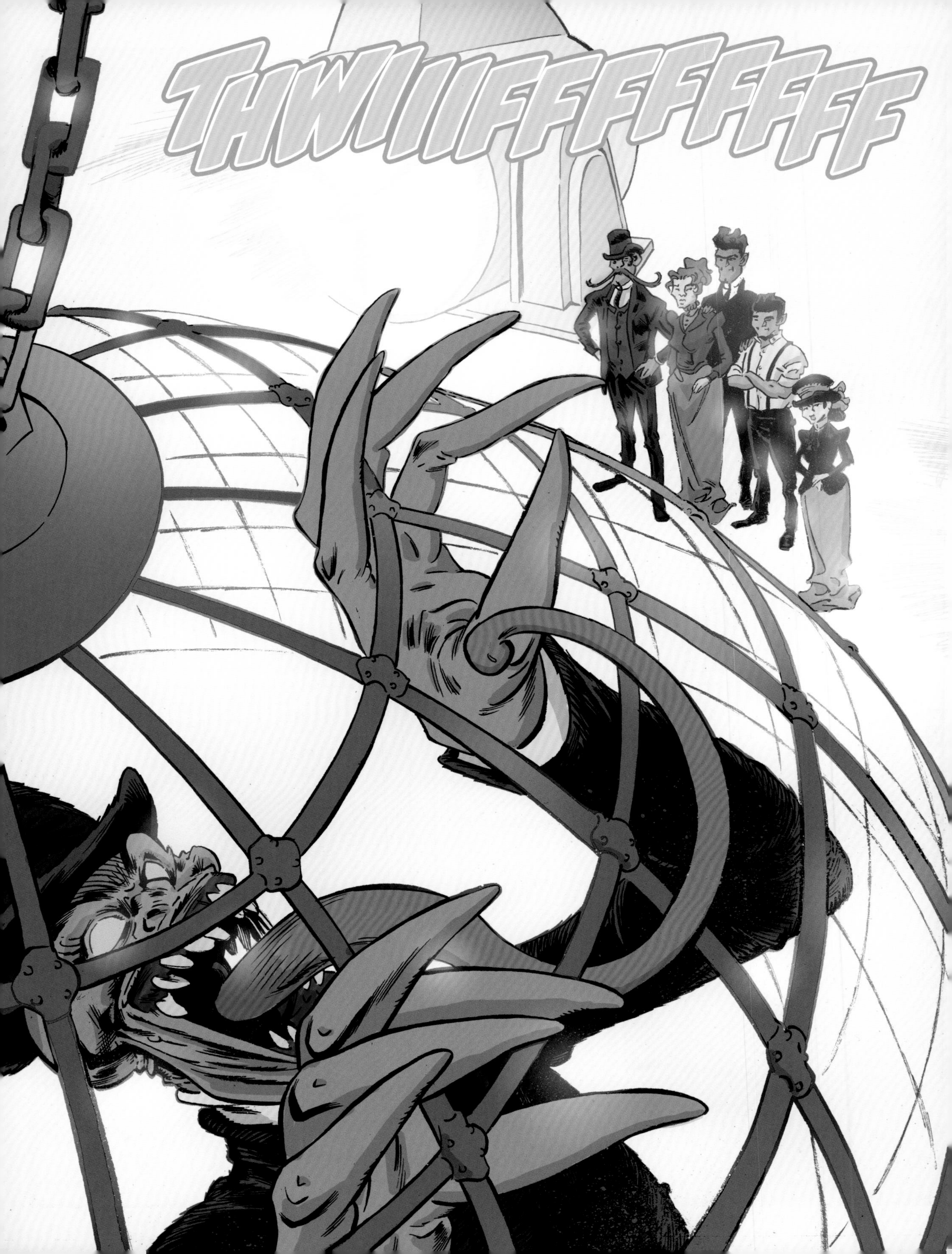
THWIIIIFFFFFFFFF

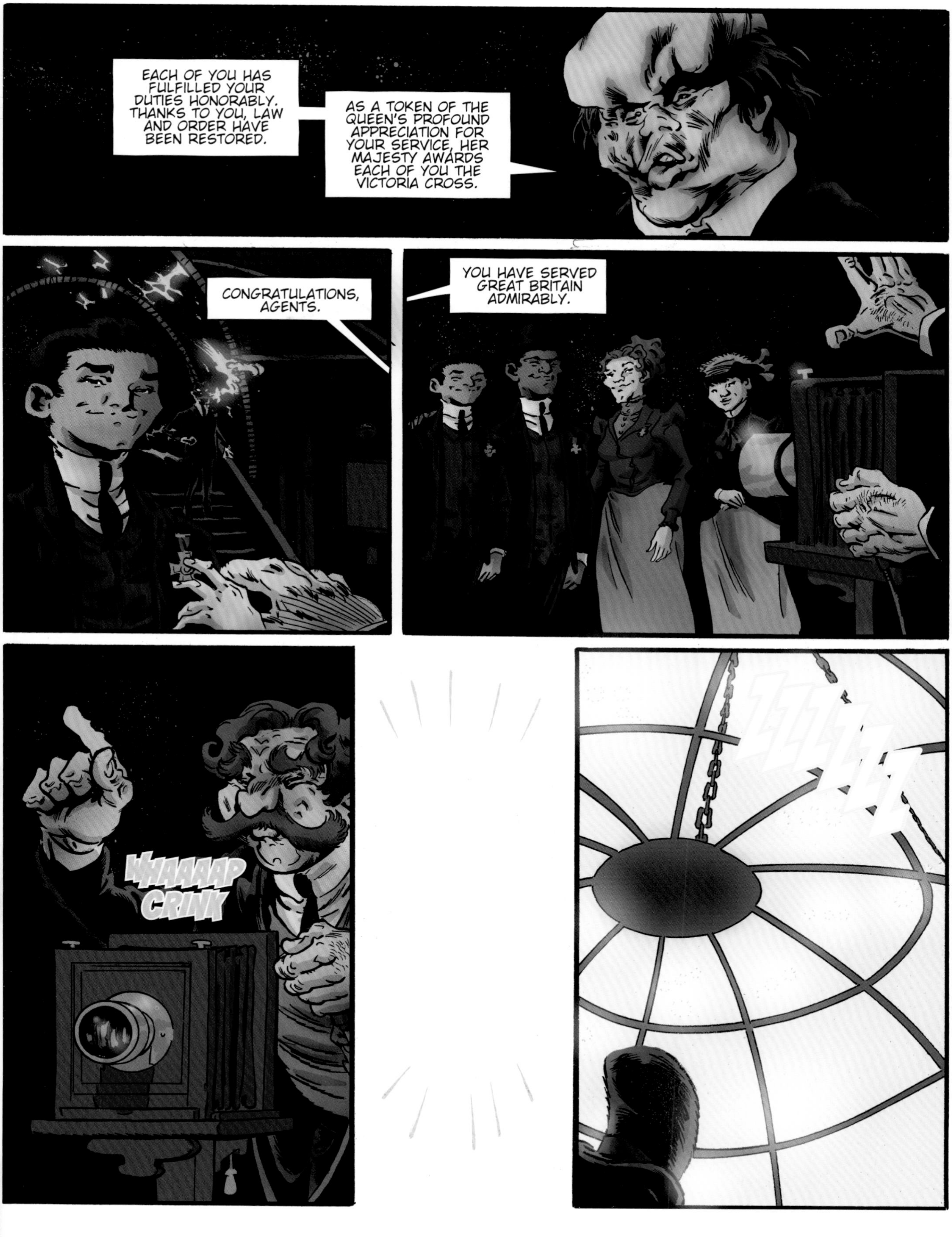
EACH OF YOU HAS FULFILLED YOUR DUTIES HONORABLY. THANKS TO YOU, LAW AND ORDER HAVE BEEN RESTORED.
AS A TOKEN OF THE QUEEN'S PROFOUND APPRECIATION FOR YOUR SERVICE, HER MAJESTY AWARDS EACH OF YOU THE VICTORIA CROSS.
CONGRATULATIONS, AGENTS.
YOU HAVE SERVED GREAT BRITAIN ADMIRABLY.
WHAAAAP
CRINK
ZZZZZ

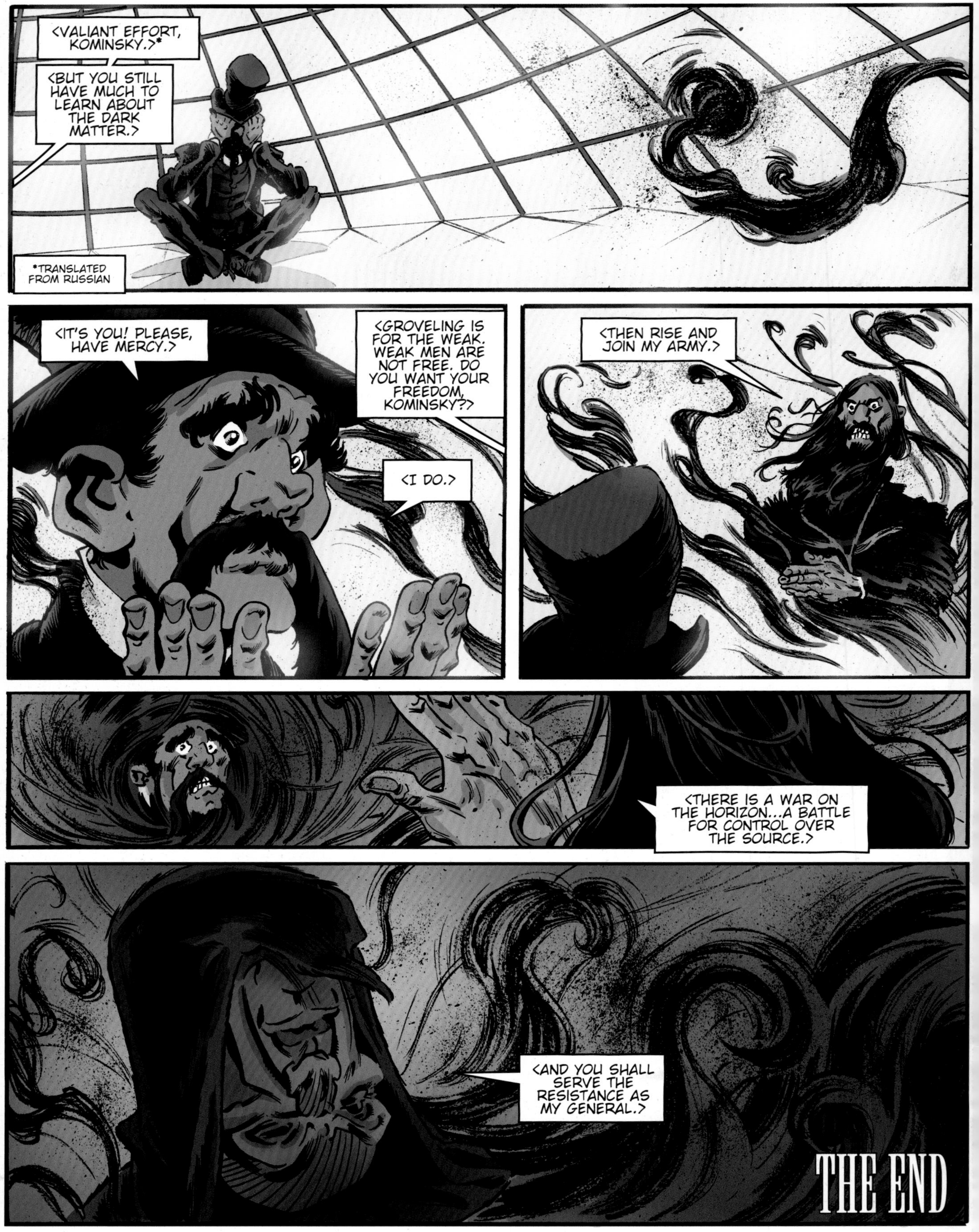
<VALIANT EFFORT, KOMINSKY.>*
<BUT YOU STILL HAVE MUCH TO LEARN ABOUT THE DARK MATTER.>
*TRANSLATED FROM RUSSIAN
<IT'S YOU! PLEASE, HAVE MERCY.>
<GROVELING IS FOR THE WEAK. WEAK MEN ARE NOT FREE. DO YOU WANT YOUR FREEDOM, KOMINSKY?>
<I DO.>
<THEN RISE AND JOIN MY ARMY.>
<THERE IS A WAR ON THE HORIZON...A BATTLE FOR CONTROL OVER THE SOURCE.>
<AND YOU SHALL SERVE THE RESISTANCE AS MY GENERAL.>
THE END

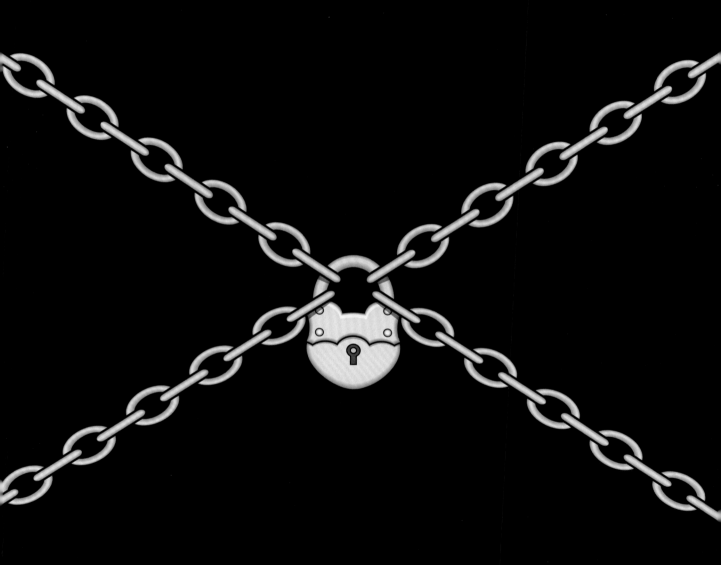

BEFORE HOUDINI

A COMIC IN THE MAKING

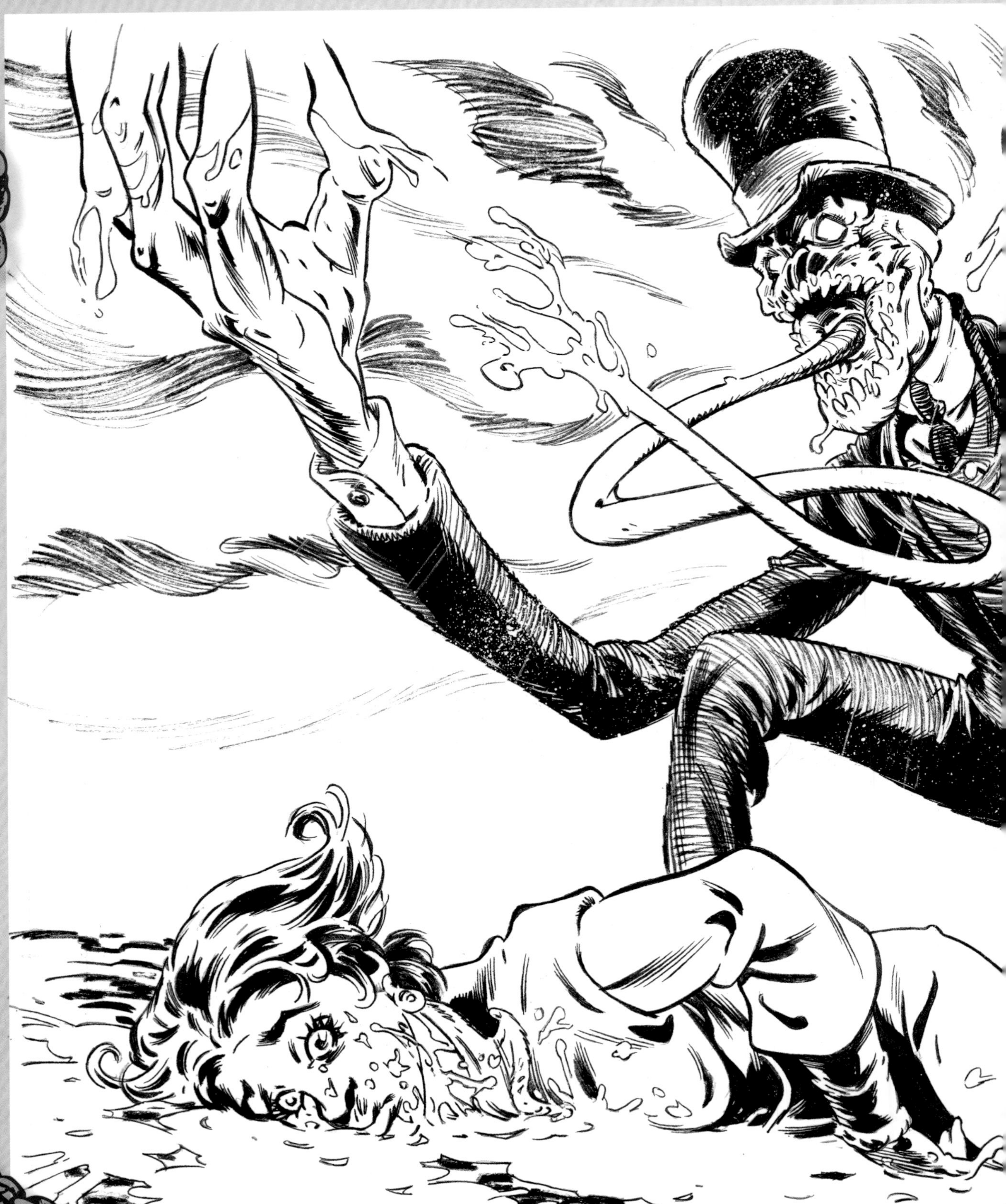

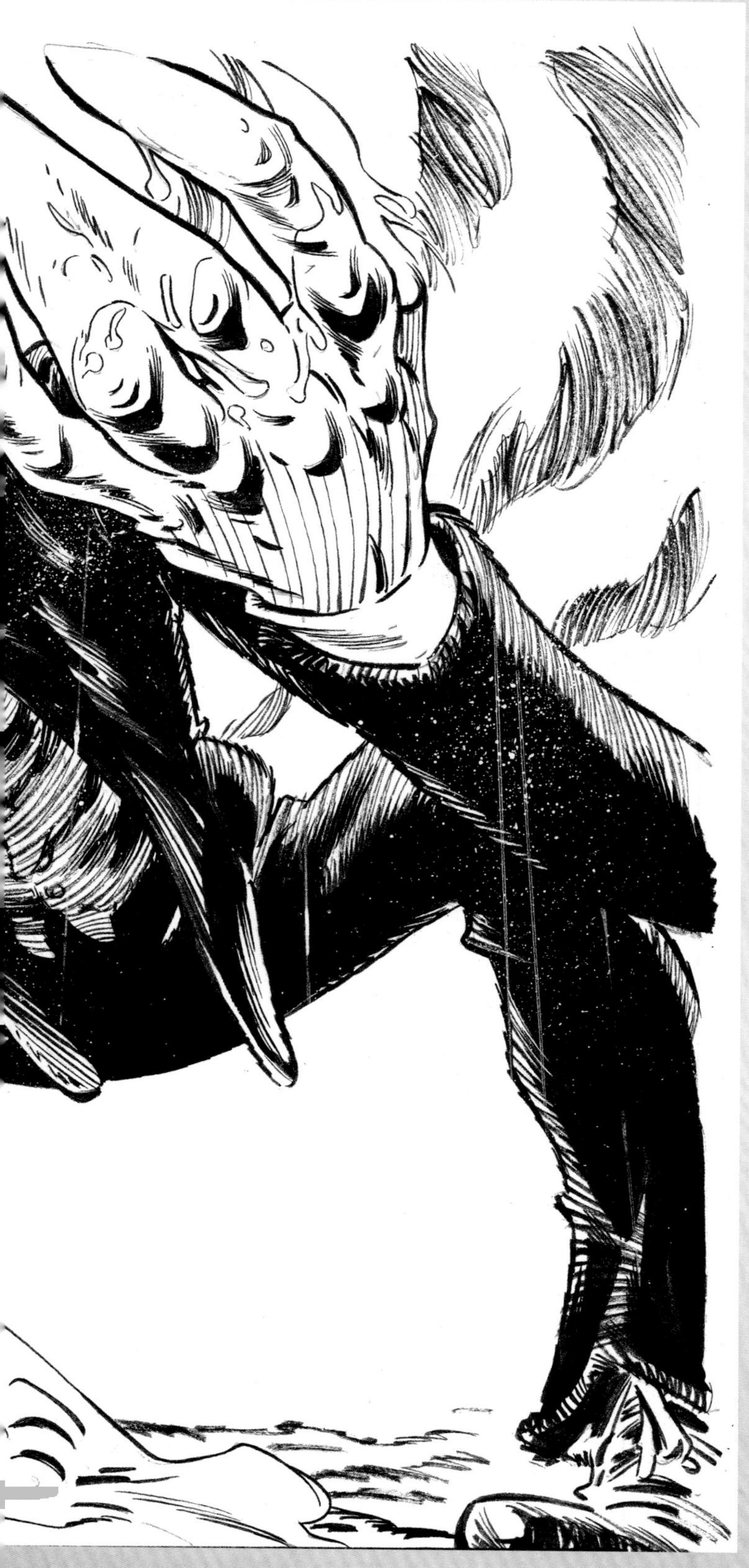

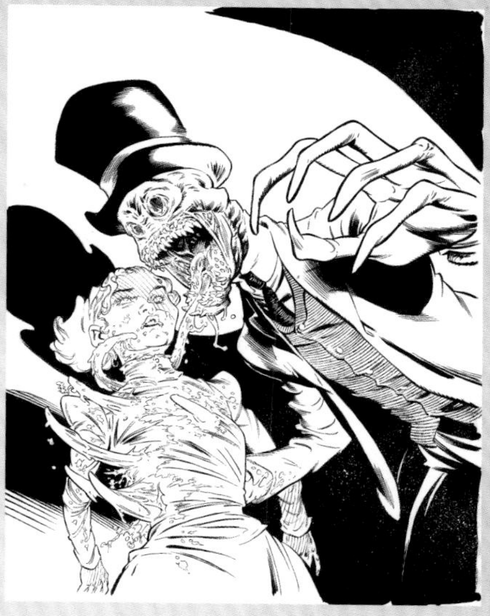

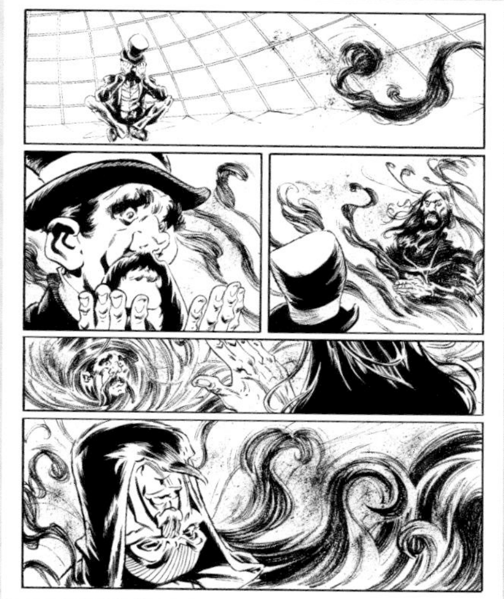

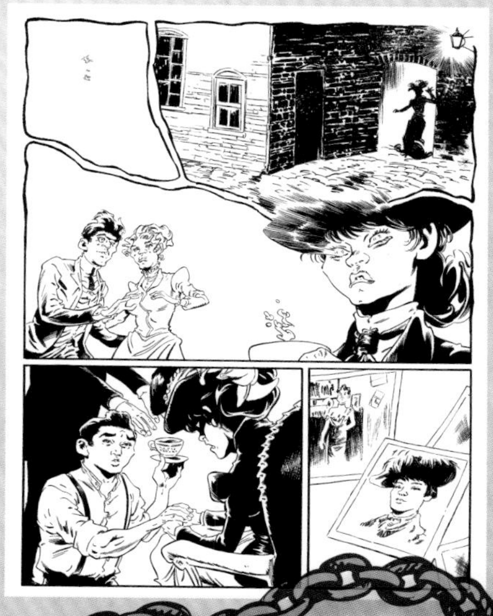

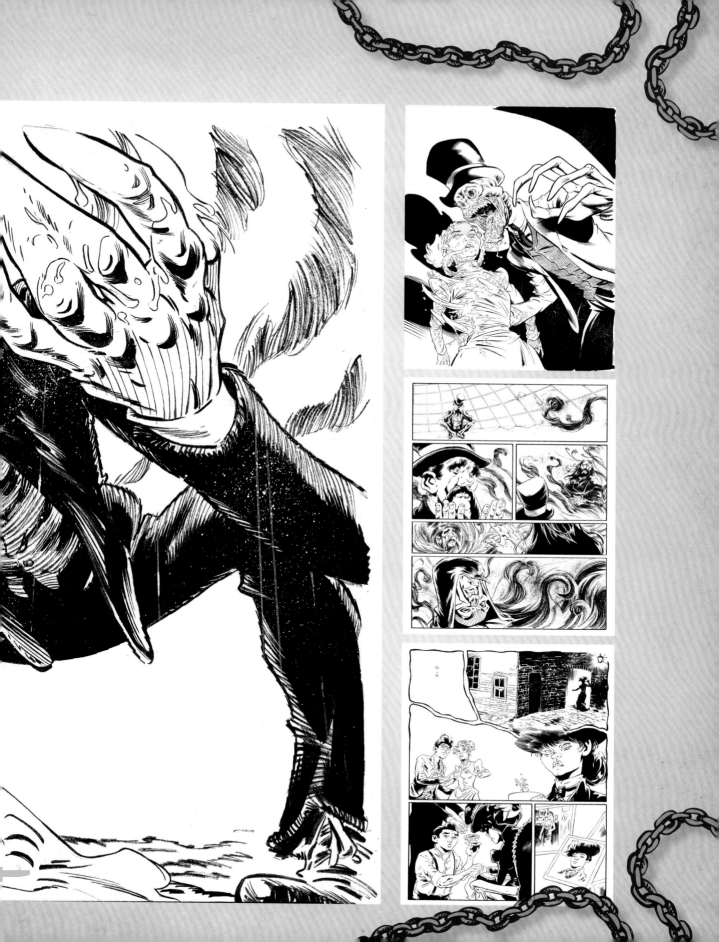

An imprint of Insight Editions
PO Box 3088
San Rafael, CA 94912
www.insightcomics.com

Find us on Facebook:
www.facebook.com/InsightEditionsComics

Follow us on Twitter:
@InsightComics

Follow us on Instagram:
Insight_Comics

Published by Insight Editions, San Rafael, California, in 2019. All rights reserved.
No part of this book may be reproduced in any form without written permission from the publisher.
Library of Congress Cataloging-in-Publication Data available.

ISBN: 978-1-68383-063-4

Publisher: Raoul Goff
Associate Publisher: Vanessa Lopez
Design Support: Brooke McCullum
Executive Editor: Mark Irwin
Assistant Editor: Holly Fisher
Senior Production Editor: Elaine Ou
Production Manager: Sadie Crofts

Insight Editions, in association with Roots of Peace, will plant two trees for each tree used in the manufacturing of this book.
Roots of Peace is an internationally renowned humanitarian organization dedicated to eradicating land mines worldwide and
converting war-torn lands into productive farms and wildlife habitats. Roots of Peace will plant two million fruit and nut trees
in Afghanistan and provide farmers there with the skills and support necessary for sustainable land use.

Manufactured in China by Insight Editions

10 9 8 7 6 5 4 3 2 1